CHURCHILL & EISENHOWER

TOGETHER AGAIN & A VIRGINIA VISIT

CHURCHILL & EISENHOWER
TOGETHER AGAIN & A VIRGINIA VISIT

As chronicled by Photographer Frank A. Dementi

and Retold by Dr. Brian A. Dementi

and others

DEMENTI
MILESTONE PUBLISHING

First Printing

Publisher
Wayne Dementi
Dementi Milestone Publishing, Inc.
Manakin-Sabot, VA 23103
www.dementimilestonepublishing.com

The Library of Congress Control Number: 2014918876

ISBN: 978-0-9909613-0-7

Graphic design by:
Amy Mendelson Cheeley, Amy Mendelson Design

Printed in the United States

CONTENTS

DEDICATION

Frank Dementi

This book is lovingly dedicated to the memory of Frank Armstead Dementi, a wonderful father, a fabulous personality, and, in my opinion, Virginia's greatest photographer, if not the best in the world............

His son,

Brian Dementi

to the memory of my uncle, Benjamin (Benjie) Sims, who survived five major battles of World War II, including the Normandy Invasion and the Battle of the Bulge. He met his future wife, Georgette, when she was pedaling out of Paris as the Allies approached to liberate the city............

and to the memory of my uncles, William Sims, who served in the U.S. Army, and James Osborne, who served in the U.S. Air Force, during World War II.

Benjie Sims

Acknowledgments

The author gratefully acknowledges the many individuals who helped make this book possible. These include (but are not limited to) the following:

Joan Green Apter, for sharing her mother's delightful letter as well as her own memories

Ramona Buford, Elisabeth (Betty) Dementi, Phil Johnson, and **Charles Nunn,** who so gladly shared their recollections of the 1946 event

Joseph and **Anne Holleman,** for their encouragement and valuable aid in matters pertaining to the Virginia General Assembly

Speaker and **Mrs. John Warren Cooke**, for their gracious interview in their home in Mathews Court House, Virginia, where we discussed the 1946 visit while examining Frank Dementi's photographs

All the staff at the various research facilities which we consulted, in particular

Frances Pollard at the Virginia Historical Society. Her incredible knowledge of resource material has been repeatedly invaluable in "informing" Frank Dementi's pictures. She introduced us to the Douglas Southall Freeman file, compiled by Dr. Freeman in a time course which paralleled Frank's career.

Lisa Gilmer at the Virginia State Capitol

Marianne Martin at the John D. Rockefeller, Jr. Research Library in Colonial Williamsburg, Virginia

Minor Wissiker at the Library of Virginia

Barbara Huddleston at the Callaway County Historical Society in Fulton, Missouri

Kit Freudenberg at the Winston Churchill Memorial and Library in Fulton, Missouri

Sarah Herguner, at St. Catherine's School in Richmond, Virginia

Allen Packwood, Director of the Churchill Archives in Cambridge, England

Rob Anderson of the Greater Richmond Chamber of Commerce, for his help with the city map of Richmond

Friends whose encouragement and knowledge forwarded our efforts - in particular

LaMont Ferguson, a former "interpreter" for Colonial Williamsburg, to whom we turned often for her "insider" knowledge

Kay Stoen, for her aid in researching those in the General Assembly with ties to Charlotte Court House

Walter Tucker for his aid in identifying former members of the John Marshall Cadet Corps, who participated in the visit

Wife **Pat Dementi,** for her help in scanning and captioning the photographs, compiling the recollections, and proofing and editing copy

Brother **F. Wayne Dementi,** for his support and encouragement of this family effort, and, as our publisher, for his photograph retouching and his technical advice

Amy Mendelson Cheeley for her artistic expertise in laying out the design of the book

A special thanks to **Dr. James Martin,** my weekly breakfast "buddy," who listened attentively for hours on end, helped evaluate countless photographs, and enthusiastically supported the book effort in all its many phases. His views represented for me a bellwether of how people in general might embrace the photographs in this book. He even located and presented me with a special edition copy of *"America Goes to War,"* a 1942 publication of the American Theatre Wing War Service, Inc., which documented the early history (1933 - 1941) of the onset of World War II in Europe and the Pacific. Much of the involvement of President Roosevelt and Prime Minister Winston Churchill was recorded therein.

Brian Dementi

PREFACE

Imagine .... two of the greatest and most inspiring figures of World War II - Winston Churchill, the "British Bulldog," and General Dwight David Eisenhower, Supreme Commander of the Allied Expeditionary Force and principal architect of the successful invasion of the Normandy coast of France - accompanied by their wives, their military aides, a former Governor of Virginia, and John D. Rockefeller, III, son of the restorer of Colonial Williamsburg .... all relaxing together in the Raleigh Tavern in Colonial Williamsburg .... and you, and you alone, are summoned from among all the gathered newsmen and photographers, to come in and photograph the event for posterity! How would you feel? When it happened to Frank A. Dementi of Richmond, Virginia, on March 8, 1946, he was, in his own words, *"scared to death,"* and he wouldn't even go inside when first called. But when he did go in, he captured some rare vignettes of these two great men, able now to relax and enjoy each other's company exactly ten months after a hard fought victory over Germany in World War II and six months after the surrender of Japan.

This is the story of how it all came about - the "who," the "when," the "where," and the "why." We will see the principal protagonists and many of the supporting players in the drama through the camera lens of Richmond photographer Frank Dementi. And we will hear from some of the participants and witnesses to the events as they look back, in some cases almost seventy years, to a never-to-be-forgotten encounter with greatness. Here briefly is the story. In succeeding pages we will fill in the gaps to complete the picture so that as memories fade and participants pass from the stage of history, the event will remain unforgettable.

ENTER THE WORLD WAR II HEROES

Churchill

Sir Winston Leonard Spencer Churchill, born November 30, 1874, made his second trip to the the state of Virginia, in the United States of America, when he was 71 years of age. He came as a former British Prime Minister, whose dogged determination never to surrender, inspired his people and brought them through World War II victorious over the European Axis powers. In his first speech as Prime Minister, he had declared, "*I have nothing to offer but blood, toil, tears, and sweat.... You ask what is our policy? I will say: It is to wage war by sea, land, and air, with all our might..... You ask what is our aim? I answer in one word: Victory....*" [1] He came as one who already had begun to warn that Russian Communism was the next serious threat to world peace. Receiving an honorary L.L.D. degree at Westminster College in Fulton, Missouri, only three days before his Virginia visit, Churchill, a guest of President Harry S. Truman, had stated, "*From Stettin in the Baltic to Trieste in the Adriatic,* ***an iron curtain*** *has descended across the Continent. Behind that line lie all the capitals of the ancient states of Central and Eastern Europe - Warsaw, Berlin, Prague, Vienna, Budapest, Belgrade, Bucharest and Sophia, all these famous cities and the populations around them lie in what I must call the Soviet sphere...*" [2]

He came as one who would rise again to the office of Prime Minister in 1951 and serve his country in that capacity until 1955. And he came as one who would later be regarded as one of the most important leaders in modern British and world history, be awarded honorary United States citizenship in 1963 by President John F. Kennedy, and be voted as the greatest-ever Briton in a 2002 BBC poll of the 100 Greatest Britons.

But when Winston Churchill, his beloved wife of thirty-eight years, Clementine, and his daughter, Sarah Churchill Oliver, visited Virginia on March 8, 1946, he came as a good-will ambassador. He delivered a brief address to the Virginia General Assembly, oldest sitting Parliament in the Western Hemisphere; he received the adulation of the crowds and celebrated victory, giving his famous "V"-for-victory sign often during the

---

[1] *James C. Humes. The Wit and Wisdom of Winston Churchill. Harper Perennial. 1994, p. 117.*

[2] *Ibid, p.131.*

course of the day; and he relaxed and enjoyed the company of other dignitaries, most notably, American World War II hero and friend, General Dwight Eisenhower, and his wife Mamie.

Eisenhower

Five star General Dwight David Eisenhower, but a lieutenant colonel in 1941, had risen to the post of Supreme Commander of the Allied Expeditionary Force by the end of World War II, as responsible for the military victory over Nazi Germany as Churchill was responsible for the "morale" victory. Under his command, the planning and execution of Operation Overlord landed 156,000 men on the beaches of Normandy on June 6, 1944 (D-Day), with six hundred ships and thousands of airplanes overhead to back them up, perhaps the most powerful force ever assembled under the direction of one man. His continued leadership held together the Allied forces through the European Campaign and resulted in final defeat of Nazi Germany on May 7, 1945.

ENTER THE PHOTOGRAPHER

March 8, 1946 brought together these two men, not for the first time, but certainly under more pleasant circumstances than at any time previously. Their trip to Virginia began early in the morning of March 8, as the official party departed by train from Washington, D.C., en route to Richmond, Virginia, arriving at that destination at 5:45 A.M. Winston Churchill traveled in the private coach of the President of the United States of America. Frank A. Dementi was one of a throng of photographers at the Broad Street Train Station to greet the guests at 10:00 A.M. So too was a Reception Committee from the Virginia General Assembly, headed by Governor William Tuck. The party drove in parade through the streets of Richmond, Virginia, to the State Capitol, greeted all along the way by enthusiastic crowds (total estimate, 30,000 people), who braved the rain to get a glimpse of their heroes. Addressing the assembled delegates, senators, and invited dignitaries, Churchill gave a twenty-minute prepared speech and received a standing ovation. The audience was not placated until Eisenhower then spoke extemporaneously and was likewise applauded.

Dementi

Leaving the State Capitol, Churchill, Eisenhower, and their entourage again boarded the train for a one hour ride to Williamsburg, Virginia. The sun came out for the rest of their trip, but calamity, in the form of bucking horses on a carriage ride, ensured that the party would tour the restored capital of the pre-Revolutionary British colony of Virginia in automobiles and by foot. After visiting the Governor's Palace, Bruton Parish Church, and the Wren Building at the College of William and Mary, the official party attended a reception at the Raleigh Tavern. It was here that Richmond photographer, Frank Dementi, who had followed and photographed the event throughout the day, was summoned from the crowd of waiting newsmen to go into the tavern as the sole official photographer or journalist for this social occasion. (Likely, this unique honor came about because of his invitation to be with and photograph Clementine Churchill and daughter Mary on their visit to Williamsburg in September of 1943.)

The capstone of the 1946 visit was a banquet at the Williamsburg Inn, hosted by John D. Rockefeller, III, son of John D. Rockefeller, Jr., the restorer of Colonial Williamsburg. A brief tour afterwards through the candle-lit Capitol Building brought Churchill and Eisenhower's Virginia visit to a close, and the party, boarding the train at midnight, departed for Washington, D.C. As they left Richmond and Williamsburg behind them, they also left behind beautiful memories that would linger on and should not be allowed to die away.

So this is their story, and to an extent, that of hundreds of others who participated in some way in this historic visit. For many of those still alive who were there, the memories live on, almost as thrilling as they were on that day - March 8, 1946. For those who were not yet born, it is the hope that this book can rekindle the interest and keep alive the memories. ■

PROLOGUE

A series of widely disparate events coalesced on March 8, 1946, to bring Winston Churchill, Dwight Eisenhower, and Frank Dementi together in the Raleigh Tavern of Colonial Williamsburg, at 5:30 P.M. on March 8, 1946. To appreciate the uniqueness of that encounter, let us ask three questions, the answers to which set the stage for the meeting of those three men, each great in his own way.

WHAT BROUGHT CHURCHILL AND EISENHOWER TOGETHER FOR THE "FIRST" TIME ?

World War II was responsible for bringing Winston Churchill and Dwight Eisenhower together for the first time. The war did not come about as a result of a single act of aggression on the part of one nation toward another, but was a war of progression that became full-blown by December, 1941. The initiation of the war might be traced to the remilitarization of Germany during the 1930's, in violation of the 1918 WWI Treaty of Versailles. During the mid and late 1930's, Germany re-entered the Rhineland, annexed Austria and Czechoslovakia, and occupied Norway, Denmark and Holland. Yet, the beginning of WWII is officially attributed to Germany's September 1, 1939 outright military invasion (blitzkrieg) of Poland, followed by the September 3, 1939 declarations of war by Britain and France against Germany. France entered an armistice with Germany shortly thereafter, at which point Germany occupied much of western Europe. The war became a full scale world war at the time of the December 7, 1941 attack by Japan on the American naval base at Pearl Harbor, Hawaii. This brought the United States into the war against Japan and its Axis allies in Europe.

Prime Minister Winston Churchill and General Dwight Eisenhower were key figures in the war's European theater. Winston Churchill had been largely involved all during the 1930's and into 1941, by which time England stood essentially alone against Germany's cross-channel invasion. Russia entered the war in June, 1941, when attacked by Germany. Thus by the end of 1941, Britain had acquired two principal allies, Russia and the United States. During the period 1930-1941 much can be documented concerning the military leadership of

Winston Churchill in resisting German aggression. During this same period, Dwight Eisenhower (Ike) was essentially an obscure military figure with the rank of major in the American Armed Forces. However, following Japan's December 7, 1941 invasion of Pearl Harbor, Eisenhower, newly promoted to Brigadier General, was tapped by Army Chief of Staff, General George Marshall to head America's military planning, and American forces in Britain. Subsequent to 1941, the military expertise displayed by Eisenhower was characterized by a marked rise in his military stature to General of the Army (five-star) (December 15, 1944), with his being appointed, in the interim (December 7, 1943), by President Franklin D. Roosevelt personally, as Supreme Allied Commander for the Normandy Invasion (north coast of France), then planned for the spring of 1944. During the period of 1942-1945 Eisenhower was the principal American leader in the European theater of WWII. Further, he and Prime Minister Churchill worked together very closely until Germany's surrender May 7, 1945.

So when it was announced in the *Richmond News Leader* in February, 1946, that Winston Churchill and Dwight Eisenhower were coming to Richmond, and that Churchill would address the General Assembly March 8, 1946, people were excited. The *Richmond News Leader* indicated there were some 20,000 requests for seats in the General Assembly, which chamber could accommodate but 500 persons. Indeed, the Virginia Historical Society estimated that 30,000 people came out in Richmond in the rain on March 8 to witness the visitors along their route from Broad Street Train Station to the Virginia Capitol. Why? Because these two individuals had been in the media constantly as leading figures in the Allied effort to defeat the Axis powers in WWII. They could well have been considered as two of the greatest heroes of the war.

Though we have various recollections of who Churchill and Eisenhower were, with the passage of time such recollections fade; new generations appear, who may know little of these individuals. On March 8, 1946, the end of WWII was about 6 months past, while post-war negotiations were yet in progress. Eisenhower, five-star General of the Army and Supreme Allied Commander in the European theater, was in 1946, Army Chief of Staff in the Truman Administration. [Note: Gen. George C. Marshall retired as WWII Army Chief of Staff November 8, 1945. (*Richmond Times Dispatch*, Oct. 11, 2009, p. E-1)] Eisenhower would become President of the United States in 1953. Winston Churchill was British Prime Minister throughout the European phase of WWII, but had relinquished the Prime Minister position to Clement Atlee about three months after Germany surrendered. Here in 1946 he was Britain's senior statesman, and an acclaimed world leader, while destined to become British Prime Minister again in 1951. Both Eisenhower and Churchill would be chiefs of state at the same time in the early 1950's.

An attempt to characterize the fame of Churchill and Eisenhower, and to establish the many interactions they had with each other during the war is consistent with our intent to illustrate that they were much more than casual acquaintances, rather very close friends, when Frank Dementi photographed them with their wives in 1946. The history of WWII and the record of the involvement of Winston Churchill and Dwight Eisenhower is voluminous. Our aim here is simply to give the reader an indication of the magnitude of the roles Eisenhower and Churchill played in WWII, and of their many interactions during the war. **[To this end it will help people to understand how our dad, Frank Dementi, as a photographer, would have viewed these men in 1946, and thereby better appreciate his contemplations of the opportunities with which he was graced in photographing them together. Churchill and Eisenhower were world heroes, who worked together all through WWII. So they were indeed "*Together Again*" as they visited Virginia in 1946.]**

As WWII British Prime Minister, Churchill had participated with other heads of state, such as Franklin D. Roosevelt (FDR) and Joseph Stalin, in several decisive conferences during the war - for example: Casablanca (10-day conference)(1/23/43) (with Churchill, FDR, and many other military leaders, including Charles de Gaulle); Cairo (11/22 - 26/43) (with Churchill, FDR, Chiang Kai-shek); Tehran (11/28/ - 12/1/43) (with Churchill, FDR, Stalin); Yalta (February, 1945) (with Churchill, FDR, Stalin); Potsdam (July, 1945) (with Churchill, Harry Truman, Stalin)[1] [Truman received word during the Potsdam conference of the first (July 16, 1945) successful atomic bomb detonation. The president at once joined Britain and China in the Potsdam Declaration, a surrender ultimatum to Japan.]

At the outset of Adolph Hitler's aggression, Churchill sought to alert his people. In September, 1932, he warned the House of Commons of the movements of Nazi Germany, and urged forthrightness on the part of the government in dealing with the public. During the period of the rise of Hitler (1933-1939), Germany repeatedly violated the WWI Treaty of Versailles (1918), and facing no resistance from France or Britain, re-occupied the Rhineland in 1936, seized control of (annexed) both Austria and Czechoslovakia, and took Norway, Denmark and Holland. **The beginning of WWII is officially dated to September 1, 1939 with Germany's outright invasion of Poland.** September 3, 1939, Britain and France at long last declared war on Germany. France fell June 22, 1940. Britain was under German air assault during 1940 and through June 1, 1941.

---

[1] *Casablanca (a seaport in French Morocco, on the Atlantic); Cairo (the capital of the United Arab Republic, in Egypt on the Nile); Tehran (the capital of Aran- near the Caspian Sea); Yalta (a town in the Crimea, U.S.S.R., on the Black Sea); Potsdam (a city in eastern Germany, near Berlin)*

In 1940 British Prime Minister Neville Chamberlain resigned, and King George VI appointed Winston Churchill as Prime Minister. His first address to the House of Commons was one of his most notable. Certain excerpts from his address serve to illustrate the power of his oratory and his inspiration for people of Britain to engage the Nazi enemy:

> " '*I would say to the House......I have nothing to offer but blood, toil, tears and sweat.......You ask, what is our policy? I will say: It is to wage war, by sea, land, and air, with all our might and with all the strength God can give us: to wage war against a monstrous tyranny, never surpassed in the dark, lamentable catalogue of human crime. That is our policy. You ask , what is our aim? I can answer in one word: Victory - victory at all costs, victory in spite of all terror,......for without victory, there is no survival.....At this time I feel entitled to claim the aid of all, and I say. Come, then, let us go forward together with our united strength.*' " (Mansfield, p. 73)

The Battle of Britain began in July, 1940. By early September, the Germans were targeting London, sending untold numbers of planes, day and night, to deliver bombs over the city, resulting in the death of hundreds and the wounding of thousands of Britons. At times London was in flames, accompanied by profuse black smoke and red skies from the burning of the city. Yet, in the Battle of Britain during the summer of 1940, the Royal Air Force (RAF) succeeded in repulsing the German Luftwaffe air assault on England. In essence, the spirit of the British people was largely fortified by Churchill's oratory, by the inability of Germany's predominantly land-based army to cross the English Channel for a marine-type invasion of England, and by the rigor of the RAF. These circumstances caused Hitler to call off his cross-Channel invasion of England in late May, 1941, and turn his attention eastward, breaking the Russo-German nonaggression treaty on June 22, 1941, by invading Russia. Hitler reasoned that Russia stood as the only remaining potential European ally for England, and that it should therefore be removed before Germany renewed further aggression against England. By summer, 1941, Western Europe had become a Nazi-held dominion. Yet, one great outcome of this turn of events was the survival of the British Isles across the English Channel from the Normandy coast of France, from which an invasion upon the French Coast could eventually be launched by the Allies in 1944. If the British Isles had not survived at this time, there would have been no land base from which to initiate a successful invasion of Nazi-held Europe. This accomplishment is largely attributed to the resolve and guidance of Winston Churchill at a time when all seemed so bleak in Britain.

Up to this point in 1941, Winston Churchill had been a key individual in warning about Nazi Germany's remilitarization during the 1930's, in direct violation of the WWI treaty of Versailles, and in leading England to "never give in" during German military aggression across Europe from 1939 until December 1941. Largely through his influence and determination to this point, Britain survived German military assault against his country. Mansfield describes the great influence exercised by Winston Churchill in rallying the British people during the German warfare: *"Following the near disastrous Dunkirk evacuation early in the war, German bombs fell like rain on England, destroying much of London and killing nearly 50,000 Britons. England was weak, vulnerable, and alone against the possibility of Nazi invasion. Yet, in that desperate hour, Churchill came into action with such force that he jolted the nation out of its numbing fear..... He strode through bombed neighborhoods as soon as the air raids ended, always joking, weeping, challenging, and encouraging. The nation took comfort when Winston and Clementine calmly walked arm in arm amid the rubble in the streets:* [Frank Dementi's photo of Clementine and Winston, side by side in Williamsburg (p.88), helps the observer imagine the two in London on those dark occasions (comment added)], *and when the Prime Minister himself slept in bunkers as so many citizens were forced to do. Forgetting their troubles for a while, men cheered when their leader publicly insulted Adolf Hitler, refused the Fuhrer's overtures of peace, or spoke of the future as though it was a certainty he could personally guarantee. Some have said that Churchill saved England during those terrible months."* (Mansfield, p. 74) As a matter of considerable relevant interest, Mansfield says,

> *"Few great leaders in recent memory have clung to the Bible as tenaciously as Winston Churchill. He praised the King James Bible, and understood its supernatural power. In critical moments throughout their lives both* ***Winston and Clementine*** (emphasis added) *found comfort and guidance in its pages. Through it the power of the Gospel of Christ has been disseminated throughout the world. No man was thought educated who had not mastered it; no nation civilized without its influence. For generations its language defined the greatness of Christianity."* (Mansfield, pp. 102-103).

This being so in the mind and faith of Winston Churchill, it compelled him to do all he could to defeat the enemies of the civilization in which he was raised, and to warn the populace of the egregious threats to all we hold dear. The remarkable capability of Winston Churchill to inspire his homeland to stand firm against Nazi assault we must accept as deriving largely from his faith in Christ, a faith probably instilled in him by his nanny during his upbringing. According to Mansfield, *"For Churchill the primary issue of the war was faith. He firmly believed that*

World War II was a battle between Christendom and the sinister paganism of Adolf Hitler and throughout the War he replenished his unusual moral courage in worship and prayer." (Mansfield, p. 75)

While Winston Churchill spent much of the 1930's trying to waken Europe to Hitler's intentions, Dwight Eisenhower was serving as a staff officer and principal assistant to General Douglas MacArthur in Washington and Manila in the Philippines (1933-1939). These many years were in Eisenhower's view seemingly unhappy and unrewarded, with little hope of promotion beyond that of his very long-term rank as major. Apparently there was much friction during this period between him and MacArthur, as Eisenhower performed his duties forthrightly, showing no fear (to his credit) of the General. Eisenhower was, however, promoted to lieutenant colonel July 1, 1936. Nonetheless, given his concerns about his role, Eisenhower requested transfer in August, 1939. (Though Eisenhower may not have realized it, these years with MacArthur were equipping him with the skills needed to deal with the many personality types who were to follow in his command as Supreme Allied Commander in Europe during WWII.)

In 1939, Eisenhower returned to the United States, where he was eventually appointed chief of staff to General Walter Krueger, commander of the 3rd army at Fort Sam Houston, San Antonio, Texas. After his successes in the Louisiana Maneuvers, he was promoted to brigadier (one star) general on October 3, 1941. To this point, Eisenhower was a little known military figure. That status was about to undergo a dramatic change over the next four years after General George Marshall, Army Chief of Staff, recognized Eisenhower's talents and brought him into key positions in America's and the Allies' defenses following the December 7, 1941 Japanese bombing of Pearl Harbor.

December 7, 1941, was a day that changed the course of the war and set in motion events that would establish the close working relationship between Winston Churchill and Dwight Eisenhower. Japan bombed Pearl Harbor. On December 8, 1941, the United States Congress declared war on Japan, and on December 11, 1941, Germany and Italy declared war on the United States. Then further, on December 11, 1941, at the behest of President Franklin Roosevelt, Congress officially recognized a state of war existed between the U. S. and Germany, and the U. S. and Italy. After the December, 1941 declarations of war, now involving both the European and Pacific theaters, there emerged a parallel elevation of General Eisenhower and Prime Minister Churchill as military and political leaders in a world-wide war.[2]

---

[2] *Briefly stated the course of the war in Europe involved Allied engagement/pursuit of Axis forces in the Mediterranean along north Africa, across Sicily and into the boot of Italy during 1942-43. The* <u>*primary*</u> *Allied effort then shifted January, 1944 from the Mediterranean to preparations for an across-Channel invasion of the north coast of France (Normandy Invasion), which took place June 6, 1944, and then on across the continent (Russia approaching from the east) to Berlin, where Germany surrendered May 7, 1945.]*

At the time of the bombing of Pearl Harbor, Dwight Eisenhower, in contrast to Churchill, was a relatively obscure military man with the rank of brigadier general. What the world witnessed post December 7, 1941, was a meteoric rise in military rank, responsibility, and world-wide military leadership accomplishments of untold proportions, on the part of General Dwight Eisenhower. By the war's end in 1945, he had risen in rank to General of the Army (five-star); he was Supreme Commander in the 1942-1943 Allied campaign against Germany in the Mediterranean across North Africa, Sicily, and thence into the boot of Italy. In the autumn of 1943, there was much pressure from world figures for chiefs of state Churchill and Roosevelt to name a commander for an across-Channel invasion of the French coast, code name Overlord. Following a very diffcult consideration of conflicting views from various military leaders, President Franklin D. Roosevelt, during his visit with Eisenhower in Tunis, personally informed Eisenhower on December 7, 1943, of his appointment as Supreme Allied Commander for the Allied invasion of the Normandy coast of France. <u>This decision of President Roosevelt was enthusiastically welcomed and endorsed by British Prime Minister Winston Churchill.</u>

After the December 7, 1941 bombing of Pearl Harbor, General George Marshall, Army Chief-of-Staff under President Franklin Roosevelt, called General Dwight Eisenhower to Washington. Eisenhower arrived in D. C. on December 14. He was ushered immediately into Marshall's office. Marshall asked the General to summarize everything of relevance to the situation in the Pacific, perhaps a reasonably directed question to one who had served so well for years under General Douglas MacArthur in the Philippines. Eisenhower's able response found favor with Marshall.

Also, in December 1941, Winston Churchill and the British chiefs of staff arrived in Washington for three weeks of talks that constituted the Arcadia Conference, the first joint meeting of the two allies. Arcadia was responsible in part for Churchill's great reception in the United States. His oratory before a joint session of Congress the day after Christmas, in which he condemned Germany and Japan, while praising the Allies, was met with resounding cheers in both houses. In February, 1942, Marshall selected Eisenhower as his chief war planner, and by virtue of this position, Eisenhower was then the defacto architect of American strategy. June 11, 1942, George Marshall appointed Eisenhower as commander of all American forces in Britain. Later, on July 25, 1942, by action of the Anglo-America Combined Chiefs of Staff, Eisenhower was elected the Supreme Commander of the Allied Force for the invasion of North Africa in the Mediterranean. <u>All three of these events in 1942</u> attest to the recognition of Eisenhower's expertise and to his huge advancement in military leadership on the world's stage.

In July of 1942, Eisenhower was called to the White House by President Roosevelt and formally introduced to Prime Minister Churchill. Eisenhower was posted to England on June 24, 1942, as head of American forces in Britain. From the time he arrived in England, the history of his incredible leadership roles as commander in the Allied campaign against Axis powers in the Mediterranean (1942-1943), and as Supreme Allied Commander in the 1944 Normandy invasion of France, and the Allied advance 1944-45 across Europe to Berlin, resulting in the surrender of Germany at the Allied headquarters in Reims France, May 7, 1945, is extremely weighty. It is the subject of lengthy biographies and historical accounts, the review of which is beyond the scope of this book. Yet, certain events should be recognized.

General Eisenhower, Supreme Allied Commander, received from the Combined Chiefs of Staff on February 12, 1944, his directive for the Allied invasion of the Normandy coast. His mission as presented in various sources: *You will enter the continent of Europe and, in concert with other Allied nations, undertake operations aimed at the heart of Germany and the destruction of her armed forces.*

The invasion began D-Day, June 6, 1944. It has been said to be the largest military invasion in history. Sources of information characterizing the size of the Allied force vary somewhat. But one estimate was that stationed in England across the channel from the French coast were some 2.5 million army personnel, accompanied by 5,000 ships and 4,000 smaller craft, with numerous convoys, 6 battleships, 22 cruisers, 93 destroyers and 7 hospital ships. At night on June 5, some 23,000 paratroopers were dropped just behind the Normandy coast.

Despite all the concerns felt and expressed by military leaders before the invasion as to its outcome, the cross-channel invasion of the north coast of France was by all accounts remarkably successful. It represented the turn of the war for the Allied forces against the Axis powers. The weather across the English Channel during early June seemed to preclude such an invasion - solidly so in the minds of German military leaders. Yet, through the diligence of British meteorologists, an opening in the weather of June 6, 1944, was detected, and when this was communicated to General Eisenhower, he said: "*Let's go.*" The weather, which posed a fearful obstacle to Allied efforts, quite by contrast became for the Allies a positive factor by virtue of the element of surprise it accorded them in implementing the invasion.

All things considered, we suggest here that the Allied victory at Normandy was Providential, in the same sense that Pulitzer-Prize-winning Southern historian, Douglas Southall Freemen perceived the American Colonists' victory at Yorktown (surrender of Lord Cornwallis to General George Washington) in 1781 in the American Revolution as Providential. Freeman said in his *The Significance of Yorktown:*

> " *The story of Yorktown is not to be read in the published reports or reconstructed from the weathered redoubts. The battle, through the climax of the war, had been won in the hearts of Americans before it was waged on the heights above the York. For the revolution was the most personal of wars. If men believed the uprising a crime against king and conscience, they paid for their conviction in obloquy and in exile. If they held the revolution to be the cause of justice and of right, then they gave to it their bodies and their belongings and were likely to lose both in the campaigns that covered the land from Savannah to Saratoga. The victory of Yorktown, to these patriots, was answered prayer, rewarded patience, vindicated faith. The triumph of their arms seemed a miracle. It lay at the basis of the belief, which prevailed in America until the War Between the States, that a special Providence had created a new nation as it had in ancient days preserved a chosen people* (see Exodus chapters 14-15; reference added). *This is the spiritual significance of Yorktown and it far outweighs the military and the political importance of that last campaign." (Freeman, as cited in Goodwin, p. 9)* (We would add that after referring to Freeman in his March 8, 1946 speech before the Virginia General Assembly, Winston Churchill made note of the fact that Douglas Southall Freeman was present in the audience that day.)

When Germany surrendered, Eisenhower signed a very brief statement at Allied Headquarters in Reims France affirming completion of his assigned mission, saying in essence, that at 2:41 A.M. local time on May 7, 1945, Germany signed the document of surrender. This document stipulated that Germany would cease fighting on all fronts within 24 hours. The joy expressed in Britain and the United States May 7 in response to Eisenhower's written announcement of the surrender was profound.

In retrospect, Admiral Friedrich Ruge, naval adviser to Rommel at the time, called Eisenhower's decision to go forward with the Normandy Invasion, made that night "without having to clear that decision with higher authority" ... '*one of the truly great decisions in military history,*' (Eisenhower, David, p. 251). It should be said at this point that before, or certainly by the time of the Normandy Invasion, June 6, 1944, until the surrender of Germany on May 7, 1945, Ike was in the driver's seat as decision maker for the Allied invasion in Europe, this despite the fact that the Supreme Allied Commander's chain of command arguably was President Franklin Roosevelt through the Army Chief-of-Staff, General George Marshall. By the time of the Normandy Invasion, if not before, the military effort was not directed by FDR or Gen. Marshall; rather they gave Ike free rein to make the critical decisions in the Anglo-American Allied military campaign in the west. It is true, however, that these two gentlemen did everything possible to support Eisenhower's decisions whenever he was challenged. Not only did FDR as the United States Chief-of-State, not direct Eisenhower's decisions, but by June, 1944, Ike was the lead military decision maker, as evidenced by the fact he related to the British Chief-of-State, Prime Minister Winston Churchill, during 1942-44, on a one-to-one basis in much consultation. Yet, where Ike, of the two, was the actual military decision maker, this was especially so when the U. S. became the dominant Anglo-American Allied nation in the war.

Following the end of the war in Europe, General Eisenhower's fame was world-wide. As an example, one source indicated that on a trip to New York in mid-June, 1945, some four to five million people, the largest crowd in the city's history, turned out to welcome him. Nowhere is Eisenhower's fame (heroism) more succinctly presented than in the somewhat brief TIME Magazine's June 6, 1994, 50th anniversary Special Report: *D-Day: General Dwight D. Eisenhower: The Man Who Beat Hitler,* which provides good summary information on the course of the war in Europe, focusing on the June 6, 1944 Normandy Invasion. It presents in text and diagrams the buildup of Allied troops and materials of warfare on England's southern coast, and the invasion of the north coast of France, across five beachheads: Utah, Omaha, Gold, Juno, and Sword. Eisenhower's competence in fulfilling this tremendous task, despite antagonism from British military leaders he commanded, is well presented. It might be said of General Dwight Eisenhower that he was not only the Supreme Allied Commander who would give the order to attack, but that on his shoulders lay the responsibility to decide when to launch the invasion. He had no obligation to wait for such a decision from his higher command (U. S. President or U. S. Army Chief of Staff). The decision to launch the Normandy Invasion was his alone.

During the course of the military campaign there were many, many instances of personal encounters and discussions between Dwight Eisenhower, and the British Prime Minister, Winston Churchill. Eisenhower took into consideration much of the military guidance he received from Churchill, who was extremely active in the military field. It is of particular interest to us to illustrate by this how close the relationship was between Eisenhower and Churchill. There are numerous instances of the personal, constructive, interactions between Churchill and Eisenhower all during the war. To establish the flavor, a few of the many examples of recorded interactions between the two are presented as follows:

- Upon Eisenhower's arrival in England in 1942, Prime Minister Winston Churchill got into the habit of inviting Eisenhower to dinner, very often at No. 10 Downing Street, and on some of these occasions, Eisenhower (often accompanied by General Mark Clark) endured long nights with Churchill after dinner at Chequers, the country home of British Prime Ministers.
- Eisenhower's chauffeur, Kay Summersby, a former fashion model in Paris, reported: *"One day I was asked along with Ike to lunch at 10 Downing Street...... the Churchills were living in the basement ....because a bomb had exploded down the street.......Mrs. Churchill was there, and so was their daughter Mary......Mrs. Churchill was extremely gracious and charming."* (Morgan, pp. 80-81) [Summersby's characterization of Mr. and Mrs. Churchill is not unlike those of Frank Dementi, as photographer, and Williamsburg's Marjorie Green at the dinner in the Williamsburg Inn in 1946. (see pp.126-129)]
- Kay Summersby also found evidence of Churchill's fondness for Eisenhower in the fact that, despite his relatively low rank, General Eisenhower was usually given the place of honor at Churchill's right at dinner parties, and he was personally escorted to his staff car by Churchill after the weekly cabinet meetings (Summersby, p. 24) [This fondness we believe is evident in Frank Dementi's March 8, 1946 "Mona-Lisa" photograph of the two sharing Scotch and sodas in Williamsburg's Raleigh Tavern. See p. 104.]
- According to Summersby, life in North Africa in the autumn of 1943 *".....seemed to consist of a round of luncheons and dinners for the most important men in the Western World. First and foremost, there was the P. M. One never knew when Winston Churchill would pop in. Sometimes his visits were scheduled, and other times he just appeared..... Once he told Ike that the reason he came to Algiers was to take a bath. He reveled in long hot tub baths, which had become a* <u>delight of the past</u> (emphasis added) *in England because of the stringent fuel rationing. The General would be invited to join the P. M. in the steamy bathroom for long talks, sitting on the toilet seat while Churchill soaked and smoked his cigars and discussed the state of the world." "Ike really liked Churchill. They disagreed on a number of things, matters of strategy and military priorities, and had some very spirited arguments, but this did not affect their relationship." " Mr. Churchill, you really had to acknowledge it, was adorable.... He was absolutely brilliant...." "He had the most fabulous command of the English language. I could have listened to him forever."* (Morgan, pp. 167-169)
- *"There were countless meetings with the Prime Minister for war-gaming sessions in which Churchill and Eisenhower went over and over all possible eventualities like two chess players with the world at stake. Usually these sessions would be held after dinner at 10 Downing Street."* (Morgan, p. 46)
- During the spring, 1944 preparations for the Normandy Invasion (Operation Overlord), Churchill reportedly told Eisenhower, "My *dear General, if by the time the snow flies you can have restored her liberty to our beautiful Paris, I shall proclaim to the world that this has been the best conceived and most remarkably successful military operation of all history."* (D'Este, p. 503) Paris was liberated by the Allies after the army crossed the Seine River in August, 1944, not long after the Normandy invasion in June.

- Around April, 1944, Eisenhower threw an all-American lawn party at his London get-away, Telegraph Cottage, for Winston Churchill as his special guest. Many notable military personnel were also invited. The party's activities included spearing hot dogs from a boiling pot. Churchill made several unsuccessful attempts, but finally to the crowd's applause, hit and retrieved his target morsel.
- A particularly touching private conversation between Churchill and Eisenhower May 8, 1944, 25 or so days before the invasion of Normandy, was recorded by Eisenhower's diarist, Capt. Harry Butcher, USNR. At the end of a luncheon with Eisenhower, Churchill, in parting, told Eisenhower, with tears in his eyes, *"I am in this thing with you to the end, and if it fails, we will go down together."* (Capt. Harry Butcher, p. 535)
- Churchill petitioned Eisenhower to be present to watch the Normandy Invasion from a naval vessel, a request Eisenhower refused to sanction. On June 3, 1944, just a few days prior to the projected date of the Allied invasion of the French coast, Churchill visited Eisenhower's headquarters and sought, again from Eisenhower, concurrence that he, Churchill, be on a ship in the English Channel observing the invasion. On the previous occasion Eisenhower, while expressing his sympathy, refused, not wanting to be responsible for the welfare of the British Prime Minister. Churchill was not pleased on the first occasion, and went away angry or peeved on the latter occasion. Later, King George VI expressed his concurrence with Eisenhower's decision. Nonetheless, Winston Churchill is to be applauded for his unswerving devotion to the cause.
- As the Allies moved across the continent, having arrived at the Rhine River, on March 25, 1945, Eisenhower met with Churchill and other British military leaders, General Bernard Montgomery and General Alan Brooke. As they viewed the troops massed along the river, Churchill exulted, *"My dear General, the German is whipped. We've got him. He is all through."* (emphasis added) (D'Este, p. 684) One can only imagine how profound was Winston Churchill's feeling at this sight after having been through the Battle of Britain and the German bombing of London in 1940-1941, when England stood alone.
- In a cable to Roosevelt on April 1, 1944, Churchill affirmed *"the complete confidence felt by His Majesty's Government in General Eisenhower, our pleasure that our armies are serving under his command, and our admiration of the great and shining qualities of character and personality which he has proved himself to possess."* (D'Este, p. 694)
- Jean Smith records that immediately following the May 7, 1945 surrender of Germany to the Allies, there were discussions among the victors as to the immediate deployment of their forces. Eisenhower favored the removal of Allied forces from Germany, while Churchill favored keeping the forces in the area until such time as Premier Joseph Stalin (Soviet Union) settled the boundaries of power and influence in the region. Eisenhower held that the Allied occupation in the region was settled within the terms of surrender. Accompanying the account

is a good photograph of Prime Minister Winston Churchill (in military garb, cigar in hand) and Supreme Allied Commander, General Dwight Eisenhower, standing together in London, said to be engaged in a postwar discussion. (Smith, p. 434) An estimated date of this photograph based upon the text is around May 12, 1945. Further, this good story with accompanying photograph, illustrates the close working relationship between Churchill and Eisenhower that existed between the two during and just after WWII. The photograph also shows the inclination of this prime minister to become personally engaged on the military stage.

- Winston Churchill died January 24, 1965. His body lay in state at Westminister Abbey for three days, during which time untold numbers of persons were visitors to the scene. As characterized by one reference: *"More than 4,000 people an hour had passed by in hushed honor, the line of somber mourners stretching as far as three miles."* (Mansfield, p. 25) The coffin was transported in the most elegant and respectful manner through London, past No.10 Downing Street to St. Paul's Cathedral, and thence to the shore of the Thames, and placed on the boat, Havengore. *"On the BBC, President Eisenhower, speaking from St. Paul's offered words of comfort: 'Upon the mighty Thames, a great avenue of history, move at this moment to their final resting place the mortal remains of Sir Winston Churchill. He was a great maker of history, but his work done, the record closed, we can almost hear him, with the poet, say: Sunset and evening star, and one clear call for me!.......And may there be no sadness of farewell, When I embark...."* [from *Crossing the Bar,* (by Alfred Lord Tennyson), clarification comment added.] (Mansfield, p. 27) Churchill's remains were moved via other means of conveyance to a churchyard at Bladon, and laid to rest beside his mother and father [See (Mansfield, pp. 25-27) for more complete description].
- Surprising as it may seem, one writer said of Winston Churchill: "His friends were small in number; but he loved and honored them, and they knew it." (Mansfield, p. 187) We believe the witness we have borne in this text clearly establishes that Dwight Eisenhower was one such friend. [So it is not surprising that when Winston Churchill found he was to be in Washington, D.C. in March of 1946, he made plans to visit Colonial Williamsburg with Dwight Eisenhower even before he scheduled his address before the Virginia General Assembly on March 8. (See Churchill's letter of February 13, 1946 in Appendix III.)]

In addition to biographies on Dwight Eisenhower, much more information attesting to the personal interactions between Eisenhower and Churchill during the war may be found in the publication of Eisenhower's official diarist Capt. Harry C. Butcher. The book's index for this daily diary cites numerous pages where conferences between Eisenhower and Churchill can be found. These often took place at dinners at the Prime Minister's headquarters at 10 Downing Street, at Chequers (Prime Minister's residence), and at many other locations, all during the war. These at times were intimate dinners, where Churchill was very verbose, often seeking to bring Eisenhower along to his way of military thinking. Suffice it to say, on these occasions, Eisenhower and Churchill became very close as military leaders, and as friends. Another good source of information revealing interactions between Churchill and Eisenhower is that of Kay Summersby Morgan. Their mutual respect and friendship is also evident in the speeches which Churchill and Eisenhower gave at the Virginia General Assembly on March 8, 1946. (see the text of their addresses in Appendix IV.)

Sources of Information

Butcher, Harry C. *My Three Years with Eisenhower. The Personal Diary of Captain Harry C. Butcher, USNR, Naval Aide to General Eisenhower, 1942 to 1945.* Simon and Schuster, New York, 1946.

Compton's Pictured Encyclopedia *War Volume, An Alphabetical Reference Book of the Second World War,* 9th Edition, F.E. Compton & Company, Chicago, 1943.

D'Este, Carlo. *Eisenhower, A Soldier's Life,* Henry Holt and Company, New York, 2002.

Eisenhower, David. *Eisenhower: At War 1943-1945,* Random House, New York, 1986.

Goodwin, Wm.A.R., President, Yorktown Sesquicentennial Association, Inc., *The Yorktown Book, The Official Chronicle and Tribute Book.* Issued by the Yorktown Sesquicentennial Association, Richmond, Virginia. Whittet & Shepperson, Richmond,Va. 1932.

Heiferman, Ronald. *World War II,* Derbibooks, Secaucus, N. J., 1975.

Hutchens, Harold L., ed. *America Goes To War, Special Edition, The American Theatre Wing War Service, inc.* Columbia Education Books, inc., Chicago, Illinois, 1942.

Knauer, Kelly, ed. *TIME Visions of Victory, America's Triumph in World War II,* Time Inc. Home Entertainment, Time Books, New York, 2010.

Mansfield, Stephen. *Never Give In, The Extraordinary Character of Winston Churchill,* Cumberland House Publishing, Inc., Nashville, Tennessee, 1995.

McCullough, David G., ed. *The American Heritage Picture History of World War II,* American Heritage Publishing Co., Inc., New York, 1966.

Morgan, Kay Summersby. *Past Forgetting,* Golden Apple Publishers by arrangement with Simon & Schuster, Inc., 1984.

Nelan, Bruce W. *The Man Who Beat Hitler, Time Special Report: D-Day* TIME The Weekly Magazine, vol. 143, no. 23, June 6, 1994 (p. 36), New York, 1994.

Smith, Jean Edward. *Eisenhower In War And Peace,* Random House, New York, 2012.

Summersby, Kay. *Eisenhower Was My Boss.* Prentice-Hall, 1948.

Tourtellot, Arthur B. *Life's Picture History of World War II,* Time Incorporated, New York, 1950.

Tunney, Kelly S.; Bertini, Ann G.; Zoeller, Chuck; Himmel, Eric, eds. *Memories of World War II,* Harry N. Abrams, Inc. New York, 2004.

Wikipedia, The Free Encyclopedia *Dwight D. Eisenhower* As printed March 12, 2014.

Wolf, Stanley R. and Weiland, Audrey (Wolf). *Ike, Gettysburg's Gentleman Farmer.* Stanley R. Wolfe and Audrey Weiland, 2008.

What brought Winston Churchill and his wife Clementine to the United States in 1946?

Prime Minister Winston Churchill had steeled the British people to resist Nazi aggression during World War II. His indomitable spirit and his vow never to surrender kept them fighting during Britain's darkest days of the war (1940-1941), when Britain found herself alone facing the German war machine of Adolph Hitler. When the United States entered the war on December 8, 1941, the day after the Japanese attack on

Pearl Harbor in Hawaii, Churchill found himself working closely with General Dwight D. Eisenhower, with whom he would become fast friends. For his inspiration and leadership, Churchill was respected, admired, and beloved. But shortly after the German surrender on May 7, 1945, the British people, tired of war and desiring peaceful recovery from the war's devastation, turned to another leader. In the July elections, Winston Churchill's party suffered a resounding defeat, and Churchill resigned as Prime Minister on July 31, 1945, to be replaced by Clement Attlee. But with his characteristic tenacity, Churchill, rather than fading from the scene, stayed on as the leader of the opposition party and continued to reiterate his concerns about the post-war political scene. However, this was surely a terrible defeat for the seventy-year-old Churchill, who was given to bouts of depression. His health in question, Churchill was advised by his physician, Lord Moran, to take an extended vacation in a warm climate. In September, 1945, it was rumored in London that Mr. Churchill might be planning a lecture tour in the United States of America.

Meanwhile, on July 11, 1945, while fishing on North Star Lake in Minnesota, Dr. Franc L. McCluer, President of Westminster College, a small Presbyterian college with a student body of about 350 men in the town of Fulton, Missouri (population 8,297), was hatching a rather grandiose plan to invite then Prime Minister Winston Churchill to give a series of lectures under the auspices of the John Findley Green Foundation. Established in 1937 by Mrs. Eleanor I. Green (an English-born Canadian) in memory of her husband, who was an 1884 alumnus and later Trustee of Westminster College, the Foundation annually sponsored a well-respected authority to present a series of lectures on a topic related to economic, social, or political issues of international concern. President McCluer mulled over his idea for several weeks (during which time Churchill resigned as Prime Minister), then began to move to make it a reality. On October 3, 1945, after securing trustee approval, he crafted a letter to Winston Churchill inviting him to deliver the Green lectures in the winter of 1945-46 or the spring of 1946, the date to be determined by Mr. Churchill. With letter in hand, Dr. McCluer traveled on October 5, 1945, to Washington, D.C., where Brigadier General Harry H. Vaughan, a Westminster alumnus and now military aide to the President, had arranged a meeting with President Harry S. Truman. In a fifteen minute session, McCluer secured Truman's written endorsement on the letter and his offer to introduce Churchill at the Westminster College lecture. The letter was forwarded to Churchill from the White House.

Winston Churchill's reply, committing to but one lecture at Westminster College, to be given on March 5, 1946, came on December 10, 1945, again forwarded through the White House to President Franc McCluer. In a later communication, Churchill declined the honorarium offered for his address, saying that he considered it simply a courtesy to Truman. It was arranged for the notice of Churchill's appearance at the college to be made simultaneously in the United States and in London, England. Thus, on December 19, 1945, the same news release appeared in newspapers in London, England, Washington, D.C., and Fulton, Missouri. Churchill would speak at Westminster College in Fulton, Missouri, on March 5, 1946, and he would be introduced by the President of the United States, Harry S. Truman. At the time of the announcement, the title of the address was given as "World Peace;" this was later changed to "Sinews of Peace." After its delivery the speech was popularly coined the "Iron Curtain" speech, a reference to that very phrase, which Churchill had used in his address to describe Soviet Russia's attempt to isolate the Eastern European countries under its domination.

Thus the speaking commitment at Westminster College gave Churchill a date and a reason for being in the United States. With the participation of President Truman, it also ensured him, even as a private citizen and no longer a chief of state, an international forum in which to voice his concerns about the political future of Europe and the influence of Communism, which he perceived as a threat to world peace. So Churchill's plans for an American visit began to crystallize. An invitation from long-time friend Colonel Frank Clarke of Quebec, to stay for six weeks at his Miami Beach home, provided Churchill the chance for a pre-speech vacation in a warm climate as recommended by his physician, Lord Moran. The visit would also allow him the opportunity, when in the United States, to lend his support to a four billion dollar war recovery loan to Britain, under consideration by the United States Congress. Moreover, the possibility of Churchill's addressing the Virginia legislature in the historic capitol in Colonial Williamsburg had apparently been broached by British Ambassador Lord Halifax in planning Churchill's visit. Winston Churchill, in a letter to Governor Tuck of Virginia in February, 1946 (see Appendix III), indicated that Mr. Bela Norton, a Vice President of Colonial Williamsburg, had been in conversation with Lord Halifax in Washington prior to January 9, 1946, about the possibility of Churchill's meeting with the Virginia Legislature in Williamsburg. Setting sail on January 9, 1946, aboard the Queen Elizabeth, Winston Churchill with a party of seven, left London, England for the United States, arriving in New York City on January 14. [1] On the trip to Miami from New York, they happened to stop briefly at Richmond, Virginia, where Churchill was photographed on the train. The very next day (January 16), an invitation was extended to Churchill to address a combined session of both houses of the Virginia legislature in the State Capitol in Richmond (see Appendix II).

The Churchill's stay at the Miami Beach home of Colonel Frank Clarke (5905 North Bay Road) included relaxing activities such as shopping, gin rummy games, a trip to a "parrot jungle," and a one week stay in Cuba, where the Churchills were joined by daughter Sarah. There was

---

[1] *A summary of the Churchills' itinerary for their United States "vacation" can be found in Appendix I.*

also a trip in February to the White House in Washington, D.C. for consultation with President Truman about Churchill's impending speech in Fulton. As the day for the address at Westminster College drew close, Winston and Clementine Churchill, Sarah Churchill Oliver, and host Frank Clarke left the leisure of Florida behind as Churchill entered the frenzied world of speeches and public appearances. They traveled by train on March 2 to Washington D. C. for a brief stay at the White House before Churchill and Truman departed for Fulton, Missouri, for his address at Westminster College.

At 2:00 P.M. on March 4, 1946, the President's special coaches, attached to the B & O Railroad train bound for St. Louis, Missouri, pulled out of Washington, D.C. On board were President Harry Truman, Winston Churchill, Colonel Frank Clarke, Inspector George Williams (Churchill's Scotland Yard bodyguard), Admiral William D. Leahy (Truman's personal Chief of Staff), Brigadier General Harry H. Vaughan (Military Aide to the President and alumnus of Westminster College), Charles G. Ross (Truman's Press Secretary), Captain Clark M. Clifford (Naval Aide), Matthew J. Connelly (Press Secretary), Leonard Reinsch (Radio Advisor), Charles Campbell (Director of British Information Services), Lt. Col. Dewitt Greer, Lt. Joseph Zimmerman, Jack Romagna, Dewey Long, Colonel Wallace H. Graham (Truman's personal physician) and Dr. Robert H. Harris (Churchill's personal physician). John R. Green (son of John Findley Green and a trustee of Westminster College) and Ted Marks (K.C.) were to join the party in St. Louis.[2] Clementine and daughter Sarah stayed behind in Washington. Accompanying the President's party or joining them along the way to Missouri, were some sixty newsmen and photographers (according to the Fulton Sun-Gazette for March 2, the largest party ever to accompany President Truman on tour). The train traveled to St. Louis, where the Presidential cars were switched to the Missouri-Pacific line for the trip to Jefferson City, capital of Missouri; arrival time in Jefferson City was 11:30 A.M. on March 5, 1946. Joined there by Missouri Governor Phil Donnelly, the entourage rode in a brief parade through the streets of Jefferson City, where 10,000 people lined the streets to see them, then motored twenty-five miles to Fulton, where an estimated crowd of 25,000 was gathered along the Fulton parade route to see and welcome President Truman and Winston Churchill. [3]

---

[2] *From: Trip of the President to Fulton, Missouri and Columbus, Ohio. Churchill Truman Day Collection. Winston Churchill Memorial and Library in the United States. Westminster College (In a trip to Fulton, Missouri, the authors of this book personally examined the archival records of the Churchill Truman Day Collection. The Winston Churchill Memorial and Library, dedicated in 1969, is housed in the rebuilt Church of St. Mary the Virgin, Aldermanbury. This London church, destroyed by German incendiary bombs during World War II, was dismantled, moved stone by stone to this country, and rebuilt on the Westminster College campus. Adjacent to the library is an actual fragment of the Berlin Wall, a tangible reminder of the Iron Curtain against which Churchill warned in 1946.*

[3] *Original projections of the size of the crowd which might descend on Fulton to see and hear Churchill and "favorite son" Harry Truman, was 30,000. Fulton had only two small hotels. To accommodate such a large anticipated crowd, town officials had requested that any resident with spare beds make them available to visitors. In fact, fewer people came than were predicted, so that the estimated attendance on the day of the event was revised downward.*

Winston Churchill (center left) and President Harry Truman (center right) stand on either side of the speaker's podium in the gymnasium of Westminster College in Fulton, Missouri on March 5, 1946. Dr. Franc L. McCluer, President of Westminster College, is walking toward the right (paper in hand) away from the podium, where he has just introduced President Truman, who will in turn, introduce Winston Churchill to deliver the John Findley Green lecture, entitled "Sinews of Peace." Behind Churchill and seen over his right shoulder stands the watchful Inspector George Williams of Scotland Yard, Churchill's bodyguard. Seen between President Truman and Dr. McCluer is Missouri Governor Phil Donnelly.

Photo courtesy of the Churchill Memorial and Library in the United States, Westminster College, and the Callaway County Historical Society

Westminster College President and Mrs McCluer hosted a buffet luncheon for the dignitaries at their home, then it was on to the Gymnasium on the Westminster College Campus, where Winston Churchill was scheduled to deliver his "Sinews of Peace" address at 3:30 P.M . The speech was to be carried on four coast-to-coast networks as well as the BBC. A little behind schedule, Dr. McCluer introduced President Truman, who, as promised, introduced Winston Churchill. Churchill's speech did indeed prove to be a significant political pronouncement, and its references to the growing influence of Russia in Eastern Europe (i.e. the "iron curtain" which was falling across Europe) not only provoked Russian displeasure, but also polarized many politicians, including members of the United States Congress. Even President Truman disavowed foreknowledge of what Churchill had to say as a "private citizen." (Indeed Churchill in his speech had declared that he was at full liberty to convey his own message.) Many would critically examine Churchill's subsequent contemporary public addresses to determine if he had relented in his views or softened his tone. (Toward that end, the Fulton speech and the other addresses by Churchill before he left the United States on March 21, 1946, are summarized and compared in the Epilogue of this book). Following Churchill's speech, both he and President Truman were awarded honorary degrees by the college.

The convocation over, Winston Churchill and President Truman returned to the McCluer home for a brief reception, where Churchill and Truman met with families of Westminster College alumni who had lost their lives in World War II. They then motored back to Jefferson City to catch their train at 6:45 P.M. The return route to Washington, D.C. was altered to allow President Truman to leave the train at Columbus, Ohio for a scheduled address to the Federal Council of Churches of Christ in America on March 6. After his speaking engagement, President Truman flew back to Washington, D.C., actually arriving before the Churchill party got in. At Columbus, the rear car carrying the Churchill entourage, was detached from the train and put on a siding to await arrival of the B & O train bound for Cincinnati; there it was switched to a second train bound for Washington, D.C., with arrival in Washington scheduled for 7:45 A.M., Thursday, March 7. Winston Churchill would have, then, less than a full twenty four hours to rest before he was off on another speaking engagement - this one in Richmond, Virginia. Train departure for that trip was 5:40 A.M. on Friday, March 8, 1946, from Washington, D.C.

Sources of Information

Churchill-Truman Day Collection, Winston Churchill Memorial and Library in the United States, Westminster College.
Chronology of Winston Churchill's 1946 Visit to Westminster College
Excerpt from Instrument of Gift establishing the John Findley Green Foundation Lectureship.
Letter from Guy Snavely to Franc McCluer, February 16, 1946.
Letter of invitation from F. L. McCluer to the Honorable Winston Churchill, October 3, 1945.
Letter to Churchill from Franc McCluer, December 20, 1945.
Letter to President Truman from Franc McCluer, October 15, 1945.
Program, John Findley Green Lecture, March 5, 1946.
Refusal of honorarium.
The President's Party.
Trip of the President to Fulton, Missouri and Columbus, Ohio.
Westminster College Press Release, January 17, 1946.

Fulton Daily-Sun-Gazette
Winston Churchill To Speak In Fulton, Missouri; Truman Coming. December 19, 1945, p. 1.
30,000 Persons Expected To Be Here March 5. January 11, 1946, p. 1.
Churchill On His Way To Florida. January 15, 1946, p. 1.
Churchill Interviewed On Arrival. January 16, 1946.
Churchill Goes on a Sight-Seeing Tour. January 18, 1946.
Have Your Fun, Boys. January 19, 1946.
Churchill Likes To Play Gin Rummy. January 22, 1946, p. 1.
Here's The Story Behind Story On Invitation to Churchill. January 29, 1946.
Kiss From Cockatoo. January 31, 1946, p. 2.
Housing Survey To Be Made For C-Day Program. February 1, 1946, p. 1.
Joins Parents (arrival of Sarah Churchill in U.S.). February 4, 1946.
Churchill-Truman Program Set For 3 P.M. On March 5; Parade At Noon. February 7, 1946, p. 1.
Churchills Leave Cuba. February 8, 1946.
Churchill's Daughter in Cuba. February 9, 1946. Back page.
Churchill, Truman Confer On Trip. February 11, 1946.
Need 500 Rooms For Visitors On March 5. February 12, 1946.
2 Mile Parade Route Laid Out For C-T Day. February 12, 1946.
Churchill Returns To Miami, Fla., By Plane. February 13, 1946.
Byrnes and Baruch To Visit With Churchill. February 18, 1946.
City Asked To Clean Up For March 5 Event. February 21, p. 1.
Announce Party's Travel Schedule. February 26, 1946, p. 1.
Truman Has Not Read Churchill's Address. February 27, 1946.
Churchill Visit To Be Covered By Many Reporters. March 1, 1946, p. 1.
Churchill On Way To Washington. March 2, 1946, p. 1.
Visitors Arrive. March 2, 1946, p. 1.
Invitation to Churchill Suggested Talk In St. Louis. March 4, 1946.
Minute Changes; Sunday's Summer Weather Brings Crowd. March 4, 1946.
"Sinews Of Peace" Is Lecture Theme. March 4, 1946, p. 1.
Truman, Churchill Leave For Missouri. March 4, 1946.
Churchill and Truman Cited. March 5, 1946, p. 1.
Churchill Warns Of Red Bid For Power; 25,000 Line The Streets For Parade. March 5, 1946, p. 1.
Churchill Arrives In Washington After Tour. March 7, 1946.
Churchill Preparing To Return To England. March 11, 1946.

The New York Times.
'Iron Curtain' Speech Recalled At Rebuilt London Church In Missouri. May 8, 1969, p. 3.

The Richmond News Leader (Blue Streak Edition).
Crowds Line Streets in Jefferson City to See Churchill. March 5, 1946. p. 1.

The Richmond Times Dispatch
Churchill Speech Stirs Heated Senate Debate. March 7, 1946, p. 3.
Churchill Speech Called Aggressive. March 8, 1946, 0p 1.
Wallace Agrees With Senators Shocked by Churchill's Speech. March 8, 1946, p. 4.
Churchill Aired Private View In Address, Commons Is Told. March 11, 1946, p. 3.

WHAT BROUGHT FRANK DEMENTI TO THE RALEIGH TAVERN IN COLONIAL WILLIAMSBURG, VIRGINIA ON MARCH 8, 1946?

Once upon a time, Richmond press photographer, Frank Armstead Dementi, established a new photographic studio in Colonial Williamsburg, Virginia. Frank Dementi's Colonial Studio was located in Williamsburg's restored area during the period 1942-1945. After World War II ended in 1945, the studio, while retaining the same name, was moved to 9 East Grace Street in Richmond, where it operated until Frank's retirement in 1984. Yet, due to the close proximity of Williamsburg and Richmond, and Frank's many contacts in Williamsburg, the colonial city remained a focal point of Frank's professional activity during his career as photographer. Throughout the history of Colonial Studio and that of Frank's career as photographer, his wife, Connie Mae Sims, stood at his side, essentially running the business of the studio.

At its inception, Colonial Studio was located on the Duke of Gloucester Street in the business section near the street's confluence with the College of William & Mary's campus. This business section was very small but lovely and colonial in character, and it constituted a portion of Colonial Williamsburg, the one time British capital in the Western Hemisphere, until the time of the American Revolution. During the period of colonial dissent, prior to and during the American Revolutionary War (1776-1781), Williamsburg was a center of Virginia's political activity. Winston Churchill elected to accept Virginia's invitation to speak to the General Assembly in March, 1946, at least in part because it was the first legislative body in the New World, and he had hoped to address the body convened in Williamsburg itself. Doing so would also enable him to visit the historic Williamsburg- Yorktown- Jamestown tri-city area of Virginia, in which he had a great interest.

In September, 1943, during WWII, Prime Minister Winston Churchill, his wife, Clementine, and his daughter, Mary, were on another visit to the United States. Mary was serving as a subaltern in the British Army but came on the trip as her father's aide-de-camp. While Winston Churchill was involved in consultations in Washington, D.C., it was apparently decided that Clementine and Mary would slip down to Colonial Williamsburg, the former British capital, for an unannounced day of relaxation. Consequently it fell to the British Embassy to make the proper arrangements.

OPPOSITE: On September 8,1943, Clementine Churchill and daughter Mary made a "flying visit" (Mary's own words) to Colonial Williamsburg, Virginia, while Winston Churchill was conducting state business in Washington, D.C. Richmond photographer, Frank A. Dementi, per a request from the British Embassy, traveled to Williamsburg, where he was assigned as the official photographer of the Churchill party for the day. Here he captures Clementine Churchill entering her vehicle in front of Travis House on Duke of Gloucester Street. This may have been where Clementine and Mary lunched, along with photographer Dementi. (The Travis House moved from the street several years later.)*

** per Allen Packwood, Director of the Churchill Archives, Cambridge, England*

Travis House
GOOD EATING

Enter photographer Frank Dementi. One day in early September, 1943, Frank received a call at his studio in Williamsburg from the British Embassy in Washington, inviting him to appear during the morning hours of September 8, 1943, at the Information Desk of the Williamsburg Inn, where someone would meet him. There was no indication as to the purpose of this visit, but Frank certainly appreciated the importance of the invitation. When he arrived at the Inn, he was received, as expected, by an individual (identity unknown), who in turn took Frank to meet his subjects for the day, Clementine Churchill and Mary Churchill! Frank was invited to accompany the two women, for photographs, as they enjoyed a guided tour of the British Colonial capital. [As it turned out, September 8, 1943 was the date that Italy surrendered to the Allies, and Clementine and Mary were informed of this while visiting Colonial Williamsburg's Raleigh Tavern.] Frank spent the whole day with them and they had lunch together. The visit was said to be "secret" (non-publicized), an aspect consistent with the status of war (the guests being family of the British Chief of State) and the manner in which Frank was summoned for the occasion.

An important question to explore would be, why was Frank Dementi chosen for this task? Frank's children, having witnessed Frank's career and having heard the stories of his photographic experiences told in social settings through the years, would posit the following as reasons:

1. His studio was located in Colonial Williamsburg where the visit of Clementine and Mary was to take place. Here in Williamsburg during the war, where he was well known, Frank took portraits of many military personnel who were passing through Virginia, photographs to be sent to their families. He even photographed some German prisoners of war.
2. Throughout his career, he had photographed many events that occurred in the Williamsburg-Yorktown-Jamestown tri-cities historic area. For example, in 1926 he photographed President and Mrs Calvin Coolidge, who appeared there for the President to deliver an address at the College of William and Mary during the sesquicentennial (150th anniversary) celebration of the Virginia resolutions adopted May 15, 1776, requesting the Continental Congress to declare independence from Great Britain. On that occasion, President and Mrs Coolidge were photographed by Frank aboard the Presidential Yacht which arrived at Yorktown for the occasion. In 1929 he photographed Henry Ford in Richmond, just before the famed auto manufacturer visited Williamsburg to review the restoration of the colonial city sponsored by John D. Rockefeller, Jr. There are in Frank's files three photographs taken of John D. Rockefeller, Jr. in Colonial Williamsburg on different occasions, one of these dating to about 1930. Crown Prince Olav and Crown Princess Martha of Norway were photographed by Frank on board a yacht on the James River between Jamestown and Brandon Plantation during their 1939 visit to Virginia, a part of their wider visit to America. On

OPPOSITE: In this picture, Clementine Churchill is being escorted by Vernon Geddy, 1st Vice President of Colonial Williamsburg, up the steps of what is likely the Governor's Palace . The other gentlemen in the picture are unidentified, but Mary Churchill can be seen in the background between two of the officers.

that occasion Prince Olav received an honorary degree at William and Mary College. President and Mrs Herbert Hoover were photographed by Frank during the widely attended 1931 Yorktown Sesquicentennial Celebration of the October 19, 1781 victory in the American Revolutionary War. Others who posed for Frank's photographs on that occasion included French Field Marshal Henri Philippe Petain, American General John J. Pershing, Mrs. Woodrow Wilson, Virginia U. S. Senator Claude Swanson and Mrs. Swanson, New York Governor Franklin D. Roosevelt, the Marquise de Chambrun, and still others. (In fact, Frank Dementi's historic and artistic photographs taken in the tri-city area through the years are so numerous and interesting as to suggest an independent publication of these contributions to Virginia.)

3. Frank was a good friend and photographer of Governor Colgate Darden, Virginia's governor all during WWII, 1942-46.
4. Because of his background, Frank could have been appreciated as not only an expert photographer, but also as a source of bountiful information on the area for Clementine and Mary as they toured Colonial Williamsburg. Given his many past experiences, Frank Dementi would have been viewed as a secure person to travel with the women visitors on their "secret" visit to Williamsburg. We also affirm Frank as an outstanding personality and humorist who would have been a delight to the Virginia visitors.

Based upon many of our first hand experiences of his stories told of the 1943 visit, we believe he developed friendly relationships with Clementine and Mary, so much so, that these women appreciated him and his humor for which he was so well noted. People relished being with Frank as he told his tales about his photographic experiences and other life experiences. Photographers have a way of being at the center of important events, meeting exciting personalities as they pursue photography. We believe the relationship Frank developed with Clementine Churchill in 1943 was instrumental in giving him the opportunity to photograph, in private session, the Churchill/Eisenhower party in the Raleigh Tavern in Colonial Williamsburg in March, 1946, shortly after the war.

A selection of Frank's photographs of the September 8, 1943 visit, made from the original negatives, is presented in this chapter. Once Frank had developed and printed all the pictures of Clementine and Mary, he wished to make an artistic presentation of the photographs to the family of the British Prime Minister. On going through his stock of albums in the studio, he found the perfect ones - some exquisite gold leaf albums he had bought from a traveling salesman several years before but had never perceived an occasion as suitable for their use. As Frank himself recounted in an April, 1971 issue of

---

*OPPOSITE: In this photograph Clementine (right) and Mary (center) Churchill chat with Midge Adolph, (left) a Colonial Williamsburg interpreter, at the entrance of what is probably the Governor's Palace. According to Mary, while visiting one of the "lovely houses" in Williamsburg that day (September 8, 1943), they were informed that the unconditional surrender of Italy had just been announced on the radio. **
** per Allen Packwood, Director of the Churchill Archives, Cambridge, England*

Photographic Business and Product News,[1] he showcased his pictures in those very elegant albums costing $30 apiece (admittedly an extravagance during the war years), and posted them to the Churchills. Undoubtably both Frank and his artistic presentations made an impression on Clementine Churchill. When she next met Frank, it was in Richmond, Virginia some two and a half years afterwards. Her husband was to give a speech before the combined houses of the Virginia General Assembly. As she was waiting to be introduced and seated in the House of Delegates chamber prior to his address, Frank was taking pictures of the event. Recognizing Frank from their previous encounter in 1943, Clementine called him over to tell him that she had been extremely pleased with his photographs from her 1943 visit to Colonial Williamsburg, but had not known how to contact him to tell him so. She thanked him for the photographs he made in 1943, while indicating to him *"My husband and General Eisenhower will be at the Raleigh Tavern in Colonial Williamsburg at 5:00 P.M. this afternoon. You be sure and be there."*

Taking her lead, Frank arrived at the Raleigh Tavern around 5 P.M. As he said on many subsequent occasions, there were some 200 photographers and reporters all around the tavern, eager for a chance to go inside where the visitors were socializing [The indicated number of photographers/reporters could be, or might seem, exaggerated. On the other hand, given that earlier in the day, some 30,000 people came out in Richmond to see the visitors; and that the principal leaders of the Allied forces recently victorious over Nazi Germany were inside - namely, WWII British Prime Minister Winston Churchill (and now also as of three days, the "Iron Curtain" Churchill) and Supreme Allied Commander General Dwight Eisenhower- along with their wives and other dignitaries - the number might not be so surprising.] Presently, the sergeant-at-arms called from the tavern door, *"Would Frank Dementi please come in."* Frank has testified he was at first too nervous to go into the tavern, while a friend with him said *"You need to get on in there."* Yet, before he moved, Inspector Williams, Winston Churchill's Scotland Yard body guard, came into the crowd and escorted Frank into the Raleigh Tavern.

Being the only photographer or journalist inside, Frank has said that everywhere he looked, there was a famous face. Winston Churchill strolled over to him, and perceiving his apprehension, said: *"I believe this man needs a drink,"* beckoning to the waiter to offer Frank a drink. As the waiter presented a tray of Scotch and sodas, Frank grabbed two drinks and hastily put them away, a measure which afforded some relief of his apprehension. But more than this, the members of the party welcomed Frank into their fellowship, making him feel at home. They then posed for the many historic exclusive photographs we are now displaying in this book.

---

[1] *Moore. "Of Ships & Snails & Sealing Wax....and Colonial Virginia, Frank Dementi - Photographer." Photographic Business and Product News. April 1971, vol. 7, no. 4, p. 28.*

OPPOSITE: Mary (left) and Clementine (right) Churchill, seated on the steps of the Governor's Palace Garden in Colonial Williamsburg, pose for photographer Frank Dementi on September 8, 1943.

Clementine Churchill (left) and her daughter, Mary (right), chat outside the Governor's Palace in Colonial Williamsburg. Their visit to the colonial capital was recorded by Frank Dementi, who was their official photographer for the day (September 8, 1943).

Clementine (right) and Mary (left) Churchill stroll away from the Governor's Palace in Colonial Williamsburg, Virginia, accompanied by Vernon Geddy (center), 1st Vice-President of Colonial Williamsburg. Mary is wearing the uniform of a Subaltern with the Auxiliary Territorial Services (ATS), a rank which she had obtained in mid-April, 1943. However, on this trip to the United States, she was technically serving as an aide-de-camp to her father. Other members of the group are unidentified.*

** per Allen Packwood, Director of the Churchill Archives in Cambridge, England*

Cast of Characters

In The Virginia Visit

THE BRITISH PRIME MINISTER

Churchill

Winston Leonard Spencer Churchill was born in Woodstock, England on November 30, 1874. His father was Lord Randolph Churchill; his mother, Jennie Jerome, an American socialite. He had one brother, John Strange Spencer-Churchill. He was educated at Harrow School and the Royal Military College at Sandhurst.

In September, 1908, Winston Churchill married Clementine Hozier and fathered five children: Diane, born in 1909, Randolph, born in 1911, Sarah, born in 1914, Marigold Francis, born in 1918 (died in 1921), and Mary, born in 1922. Soon after Mary's birth, the Churchills bought Chartwell, a country mansion which served as their home until his death in 1965.

As a young man, Churchill served as an army officer in British India and the Sudan and acted as a war correspondent in the Second Boer War. Before and during World War I , he was First Lord of the Admiralty, and after the war he served, like his father, as Chancellor of the Exchequer.

At the outset of World War II, Churchill was again appointed First Lord of the Admiralty and served as a member of the War Cabinet. With the resignation of Neville Chamberlain, King George VI asked Churchill to become Prime Minister. He assumed that position on May 10, 1940, and served until July 26, 1945. His dogged determination and refusal to accept an armistice with Germany during the dark days of the war fueled the British resolve to fight on. The sight of Winston and his wife Clementine walking hand in hand through the bombed rubble in the streets of London was inspirational, as were his speeches and radio broadcasts. In his first address as Prime Minister, he had declared, *"I have nothing to offer but blood, toil, tears, and sweat: You ask what is our policy? I will say: It is to wage war by sea, land, and air, with all our might. You ask what is our aim? I can answer in one word: Victory."* And indeed, his often-flashed "V-for-victory" hand sign in effect became his trademark.

After the war in Europe ended, in the 1945 general election, Churchill's Conservative Party was voted out of office but Churchill stayed on as the Leader of the Opposition. In 1951 he was returned to the post of Prime Minister, a position he resigned in 1955. He was made an knight of the Garter by Queen Elizabeth II in 1953. Ill health following a series of strokes prevented Churchill from being present to accept honorary citizenship of the United States in 1963. Following his death from a stroke on January 24, 1965, he was given a state funeral at St. Paul's Cathedral, which was attended by Queen Elizabeth and in which he was eulogized by his war-time associate and close friend, Dwight D. Eisenhower. In his lifetime, Winston Churchill won the Nobel Prize in Literature, based in part on his six volume series, *The Second World War,* and his four volume *A History of the English-Speaking People.* After his death, he was named "The Greatest Briton of All Time" in a 2002 BBC poll.

Source: Wikipedia.org . Winston Spencer Churchill

The General

Dwight David Eisenhower was born in Dennison, Texas, on October 14, 1890, the third of the seven sons of David Jacob Eisenhower and Virginia-born Ida Elizabeth Stover. His family moved to Abilene, Kansas when Dwight was two years old. He graduated from Abilene High School in 1909 and was appointed to the United States Military Academy at West Point in 1911, graduating in 1915.

On July 1, 1916, Dwight Eisenhower married Mamie Geneva Doud. Their first son, Doud Dwight, was born in 1917, but died of scarlet fever in 1921. A second son, John Sheldon Doud, was born in 1922. Like his father, John attended West Point and graduated on D-Day, June 6, 1944. During World War I, Eisenhower was posted to Fort Levenworth, Kansas, Camp Meade, Maryland, and Camp Colt, in Gettysburg, Pennsylvania, where he trained tank crews. He never saw action overseas. At the outset of World War II, Eisenhower, with the rank of Brigadier General, was assigned to the General Staff in Washington, D.C. His first overseas responsibilities came with his appointment in June, 1942, to be Commander, General, European Theater of Operations, followed by his additional appointment in November, 1942, as Supreme Commander, Allied Expeditionary Force of the North African Theater of Operations. In the latter capacity Eisenhower, now a four-star general, oversaw the successful invasion of Sicily. December, 1943 brought Eisenhower's appointment by President Franklin Roosevelt as Supreme Allied Commander of the Allied Expeditionary Force, charged with the planning and execution of "Operation Overlord," (the D-Day invasion of Europe, which began on the coast of Normandy on June 6, 1944 and culminated in the defeat and surrender of Germany on May 7, 1945). He ended World War II with the rank of General of the Army with its five-star insignia.

Eisenhower

After the German surrender, Eisenhower served as Military Governor of the U.S. Occupation Zone until he returned to Washington, D.C. in November, 1945, to replace General George Marshall as Army Chief of Staff. His later career years saw him as President of Columbia University (1948 - 1953), first Supreme Commander of NATO (1951 - 1952) and President of the United States (1953 - 1961). Among his accomplishments as U.S. President were the launching of the Interstate Highway System, the formation of the National Aeronautic and Space Administration (NASA), and the ending of the Korean War (July, 1953).

Dwight and Mamie Eisenhower retired to their family farm in Gettysburg, Pennsylvania. He died of congestive heart failure on March 28, 1969. His body lay in state in the Capitol Rotunda in Washington, D.C. and his funeral took place in the National Cathedral. Then President Richard Nixon said of Eisenhower, *"Some men are considered great because they lead great armies or they lead powerful nations. For eight years now, Dwight Eisenhower has neither commanded an army nor led a nation; and yet he remained through his final days the world's most admired and respected man, truly the first citizen of the world."*

Source: Wikipedia.org. Dwight D. Eisenhower

THE PHOTOGRAPHER

Frank Armstead Dementi was born in Richmond, Virginia on June 9, 1905, the son of Antonio Dementi of Lucca, Italy, and his second wife, Emily Whiteside. He grew up near Sandston, Virginia, where his father owned a grocery store on Nine Mile Road, and attended

Dementi

Glen Echo Elementary School and Highland Springs High School. He later studied at the Winona School of Photography in Indiana.

Frank's unofficial career in photography began in the 1920's, when a picture he had snapped of an automobile accident on Nine Mile Road was used in the Richmond newspaper. Subsequently, he began working around the new Dementi Studio formed by his brother, Tony Dementi, and partner, William Faris, but he left after about three years to work for the Richmond News Leader. It was one day while on a story in Williamsburg, that Frank asked one of the officials of the Colonial Williamsburg restoration if they wouldn't like to have an official photographer. Their affirmative answer led Frank to open up his own studio, appropriately named Colonial Studio, on Duke of Gloucester Street on June 9, 1942. There, during World War II, he photographed many soldiers and sailors based in the area, as well as some German prisoners of war.

After the war Frank returned to Richmond, relocating his Colonial Studio to 9 East Grace Street, where, with the invaluable help of his wife, Connie Sims Dementi, he continued in the photographic business until his retirement on February 29, 1984. During a notable career, he photographed numerous historical personalities and celebrities, such as Charles Lindbergh, Henry Ford, Franklin Roosevelt, Calvin Coolidge, General Dwight Eisenhower, Winston Churchill, Admiral Chester Nimitz, Queen Elizabeth II, Crown Prince Olaf of Norway, Marshal Henri Philippe Petain, General John Pershing, Lady Astor, Lord Louis Mountbatten, Mary Pickford, and Martha Scott. He was a pioneer in color photography, and shot hundreds of color transparencies, many of which were used by the Virginia Travel Council and others to promote tourism in the state. His photos won awards from the Virginia Professional Photographers Association and the Printing Industry of America, and his work appeared in a U.S. exhibit of the International Photo Festival during the 1950's. His award-winning photograph of models in colonial costumes, made in Colonial Williamsburg and entitled "The Sabbath," was featured on the cover of the May-June, 1955 issue of Ansconian magazine.

Upon his retirement, Frank donated over 77,000 photographs, chronicling forty years of Richmond life, to the Valentine Museum. His historic personalities collection and other artistic works were given to his sons, Dr. Brian Armstead Dementi, and Frank Wayne Dementi, prior to his death in June, 1986. His color transparency collection also remains in the family.

OTHER NOTABLE FIGURES IN THE VIRGINIA VISIT

Clementine Hozier Churchill
Wife of Winston Churchill

Sarah Churchill Oliver
Daughter of Winston Churchill

Mamie Doud Eisenhower
Wife of General Dwight Eisenhower

Field Marshal Sir Henry Maitland Wilson
Chief of the British Joint Mission in Washington D.C.

William Munford Tuck
Governor of Virginia

Kenneth Chorley
President of Colonial Williamsburg
Host of the Raleigh Tavern reception

John D. Rockefeller, III
Host of the Williamsburg Inn Dinner

Inspector George Williams
Scotland Yard
Churchill's bodyguard

THE VIRGINIA VISIT, MARCH 8, 1946
SUPPORTING CAST

The Official Churchill-Eisenhower Party

Arriving by train from Washington, D.C.

Winston Spencer Churchill, Prime Minister of Great Britain, 1940-1945, 1951-1955

Clementine Hozier Churchill, wife of Winston Churchill

Sarah Churchill Oliver, 2nd daughter of Clementine and Winston Churchill

General Dwight David Eisenhower, Supreme Allied Commander, WWII, 1944-1945; Army Chief of Staff, 1945 - 1948; President of the United States, 1953-1961

Mamie Doud Eisenhower, wife of General Dwight Eisenhower

Field Marshal Sir Henry Maitland Wilson, Supreme Allied Commander in the Mediterranean, 1944-1945; Chief of the British Joint Mission in Washington, D.C., 1945-1947

Harold Braham, British Consul in Baltimore

Mrs. Harold Braham

Captain C. Craig Cannon, Aide to General Dwight Eisenhower

Major John Miller, Aide to Field Marshal Sir Henry Maitland Wilson

Charles Campbell, Director of British Information Services

Note: Inspector George Williams of Scotland Yard, Churchill's bodyguard, while not ever listed, was omnipresent wherever Churchill appeared.

16 British and American journalists accompanied the party.

[British Ambassador Lord Halifax and his wife were to be part of the party, but Lord Halifax's health (a relapse of the flu) precluded their making the trip]

Joining the group at the train in Richmond at Broad Street Station

James Guthrie, O.B.E., British Consul in Norfolk
Mrs. James Guthrie (?) (invited but not actually mentioned in records of the day or identified in any pictures)

Joining the entourage in Richmond for the trip to Williamsburg

Mrs. Eva Tuck, wife of current Virginia Governor, William M. Tuck
Colgate Darden, Governor of Virginia, 1942-1946
Mrs Constance Darden, wife of former Governor Colgate Darden

A press car for journalists and photographers was attached to the special Williamsburg-bound train. In Williamsburg, Press Headquarters were set up in the Game Room of the Williamsburg Lodge, where reporters were guests of Colonial Williamsburg at a buffet luncheon and dinner.

Joining the entourage in Williamsburg for a tour of the restored area

John D. Rockefeller, III, son of philanthropist John D. Rockefeller, Jr., who funded the restoration of Colonial Williamsburg
Mrs. Blanchette Rockefeller, wife of John D. Rockefeller, III
Kenneth Chorley, President of Colonial Williamsburg
Mrs. Jean Chorley, wife of Kenneth Chorley
Vernon M. Geddy, First Vice-President of Colonial Williamsburg
Bela W. Norton, Vice-President of Colonial Williamsburg and coordinator of activities in Richmond and Williamsburg
A. Edward Kendrew, Vice-President of Colonial Williamsburg
Edward P. Alexander, Director of Education for Colonial Williamsburg
T. Rutherford Goodwin, Director of Interpretation for Colonial Williamsburg
James L. Coger, Curator for Colonial Williamsburg

Richmond Arrangements Committee of the Virginia General Assembly

Delegate **Edward O. McCue, Jr.,** Chairman (representing Albemarle and Green Counties and the city of Charlottesville)
Senator **Graham Goode,** Vice-Chairman (8th Senatorial District)
Delegate **John Warren Cooke,** Secretary (Gloucester, Mathews, and Middlesex Counties)
Senator **Harry Carter Stuart** (18th Senatorial District)
Senator **Lloyd Usilton Noland** (33rd Senatorial District)
Delegate **Harry B. Davis** (Princess Anne County)
Delegate **George Edmond Massie** (City of Richmond)
Delegate **William H. Irvine** (Campbell County)

Richmond Reception Committee

William Munford Tuck, Governor of Virginia, 1946-1950, Chairman
Lewis Preston Collins, Lieutenant Governor of Virginia, 1946-1950, President of the Senate
Thomas Bahnson Stanley, Speaker of the House of Delegates
(Henry County and the city of Martinsville)
Robert O. Norris, Jr., President pro tempore of the Senate (30th Senatorial District)
Senator **Robert Kincaid Brock** (9th Senatorial District)
Senator **John Stewart Battle** (26th Senatorial District)
Delegate **George Alvin Massenburg,** Floor Leader of the House of Delegates (Elizabeth City County and the city of Hampton)
Delegate **E. Blackburn Moore** (Clarke and Frederick counties and the city of Winchester)
Delegate **John Benjamin Spiers** (Montgomery County and the city of Radford)
Delegate **Stuart Bland Campbell** (Wythe County)
Delegate **John Hannah Daniel** (Charlotte and Prince Edward Counties)
William Herbert, Mayor of Richmond
S. Gardner Waller, Virginia Adjutant-General

Williamsburg Reception Committee

Channing Hall, Mayor of Williamsburg
Dr. H.M. Stryker, City Councilman
Lloyd H. Williams, City Councilman
John G. Warburton, City Councilman
Vincent D. McManus, City Councilman
W. R. Woodbury, Williamsburg City Manager

Guests at the Reception at the Raleigh Tavern

Winston Churchill
Clementine Churchill
Sarah Churchill Oliver
General Dwight D. Eisenhower
Mamie Eisenhower
Field Marshal Sir Henry Maitland Wilson
Mr. and Mrs. Harold Braham
Mr. and Mrs.(?) James Guthrie
Mr. and Mrs. Colgate Darden
Mrs. William (Eva) Tuck
Captain C. Craig Cannon
Major John Miller
Charles Campbell
Mr. and Mrs. John D. Rockefeller, III

Mr. Kenneth Chorley and Jean Chorley (hosts)
Vernon Geddy
A. Edward Kendrew
Bela W. Norton
Edward P. Alexander
T. Rutherford Goodwin
James L. Coger

<u>Guest List for the Rockefeller dinner at the Williamsburg Inn</u>

The Right Honorable Winston Churchill
Clementine Churchill
Sarah Churchill Oliver
General Dwight Eisenhower
Mamie Eisenhower
Field Marshal Sir Henry Maitland Wilson
John D. Rockefeller, III and Mrs. Blanchette Rockefeller (hosts)
Mrs. William (Eva) Tuck
Colgate Darden and Mrs. Darden
Harold Braham and Mrs. Braham
James Guthrie, O.B.E. and Mrs. Guthrie (?)
Charles Campbell
Kenneth Chorley and Mrs. Chorley
Vernon Geddy and Mrs. Geddy
A.E. Kendrew and Mrs. Kendrew
B.W. Norton and Mrs. Norton

Mayor Channing Hall and Mrs. Hall

Captain C. Craig Cannon

Major John Miller

Dr. John E. Pomfret, President of the College of William and Mary, 1941-1959 and **Mrs. Sara Pomfret**

Judge Frank Armistead of the Circuit Court and **Mrs. Armistead**

George P. Coleman, a Williamsburg banker, and **Mrs. Coleman**

Mrs. W. A. R. Goodwin, wife of the late Dr. W. A. R. Goodwin (instigator of the Colonial Williamsburg restoration project)

Mrs. Marjorie Green, * wife of John D. Green, who was in charge of the dinner at the Williamsburg Inn (a last-minute replacement, perhaps for Mrs. James Guthrie ?)

* Her delightful personal recollection of the dinner, in the form of a letter to her parents, can be found on pp. 126-129.

The audience in the House of Delegates Chamber at the Virginia Capitol, March 8, 1946
(Per House document No. 25, Journal of the Joint Assembly of the General Assembly of the Commonwealth of Virginia, March 8, 1946, p. 6)
(reading left to right)

1 Inspector George Williams
2 House Journal Clerk A. D. Livesay
3 Governor William Tuck
4 House Speaker Thomas Stanley
5 Lieutenant Governor Preston Collins
6 Delegate Edward McCue
7 Assistant House Clerk George Rich
8 House Reading Clerk Wallace Clark
P House and Senate Pages
9 House Clerk E. Griffith Dodson
10 Field Marshal Sir Henry Maitland Wilson
11 Winston Spencer Churchill
12 General Dwight D. Eisenhower
13 Senate Clerk E.R. Combs
P House and Senate pages
14 Captain C. Craig Cannon
15 Major John Miller
16 Chief Justice Preston W. Campbell
17 Associate Justice Henry W. Holt
18 Associate Justice Edward W. Hudgins
19 Associate Justice Herbert B. Gregory
20 Associate Justice George L. Browning
21 Associate Justice John W. Eggleston
22 Associate Justice Claude V. Spratley
23 Attorney General Abram P. Staples
24 Mrs. Staples
25 Dr. Coleman
26 State Corporation Commissioner Downs
27 Unidentified
28 Mrs. Winn
29 Mr. James Guthrie
30 Mr. Harold Braham
31 Mr. Charles Campbell
32 Mrs. Thomas Stanley
33 Mrs. Harold Braham
34 Sarah Churchill Oliver
35 Mamie Eisenhower
36 Mrs. William Tuck
37 Clementine Churchill
38 Senator Robert Brock
39 Senator John Battle
40 U.S. Senator Harry Byrd
41 Former Governor George Peery
42 Mrs. George Peery
43 Former Governor Colgate Darden
44 Mrs. Colgate Darden
45 Richmond Mayor William Herbert
46 Mrs. William Herbert
47 Mrs. John Garland Pollard, wife of deceased Governor Pollard
48 Mrs. A .J. Montague, wife of deceased Governor Montague
49 Mrs. E. Lee Trinkle, wife of deceased Governor Trinkle
50 Mrs. Dillon
51 Industrial Commissioner Downs
52 Industrial Commissioner Robinson
53 Dr. Alley
54 House Floor Leader Alvin Massenburg
55 Delegate John Spiers
56 Mr. Bland (M.C.)
57 Delegate Edmund DeJarnette
58 Mr. Daughton (M.C.)
59 Delegate E. Blackburn Moore
60 Delegate Stuart Campbell
61 Senator Robert Norris
62 Delegate Charles Louderback
63 Unidentified

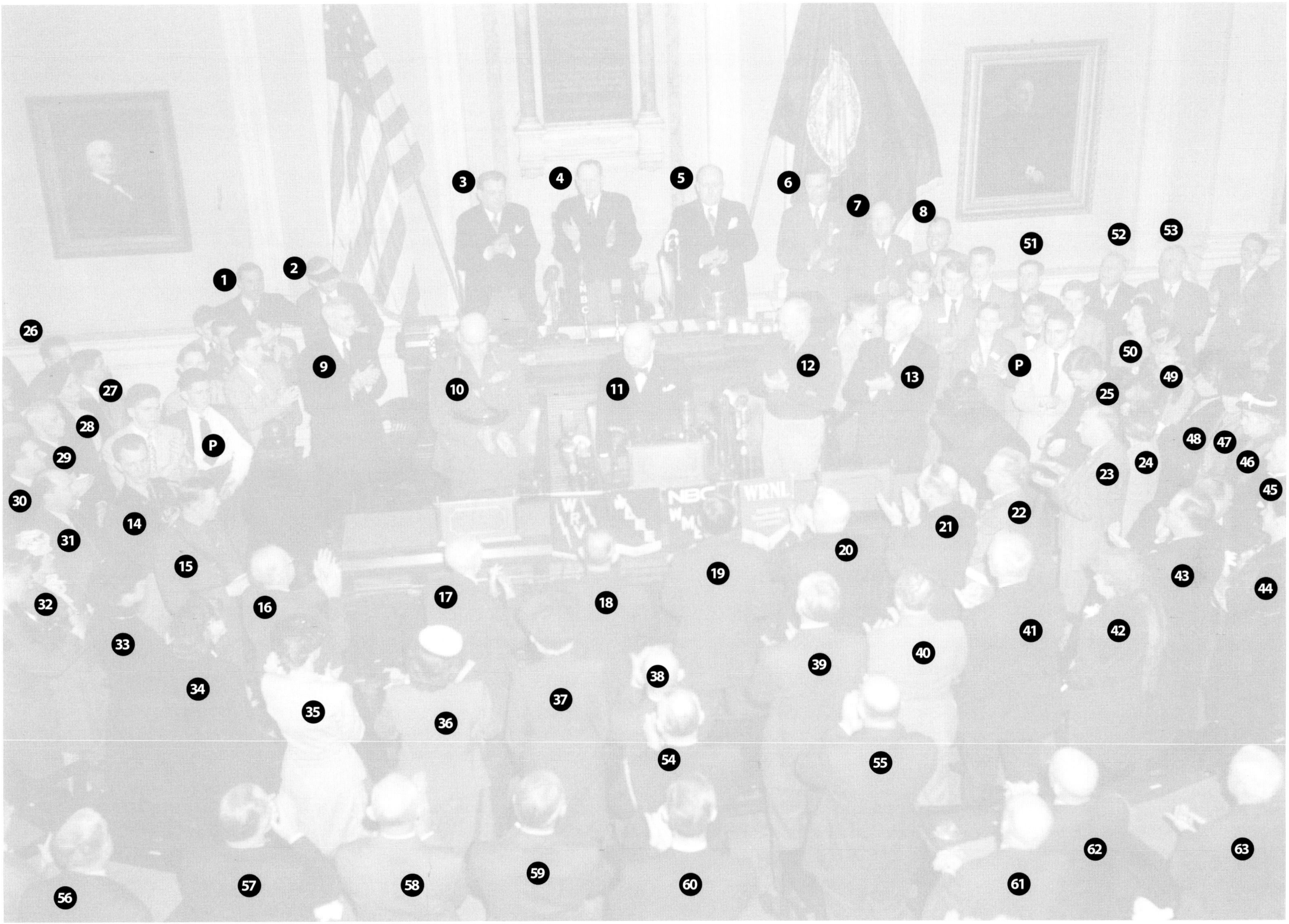

Compare this numbered image with actual photograph on page 45.

NBC
WRNL

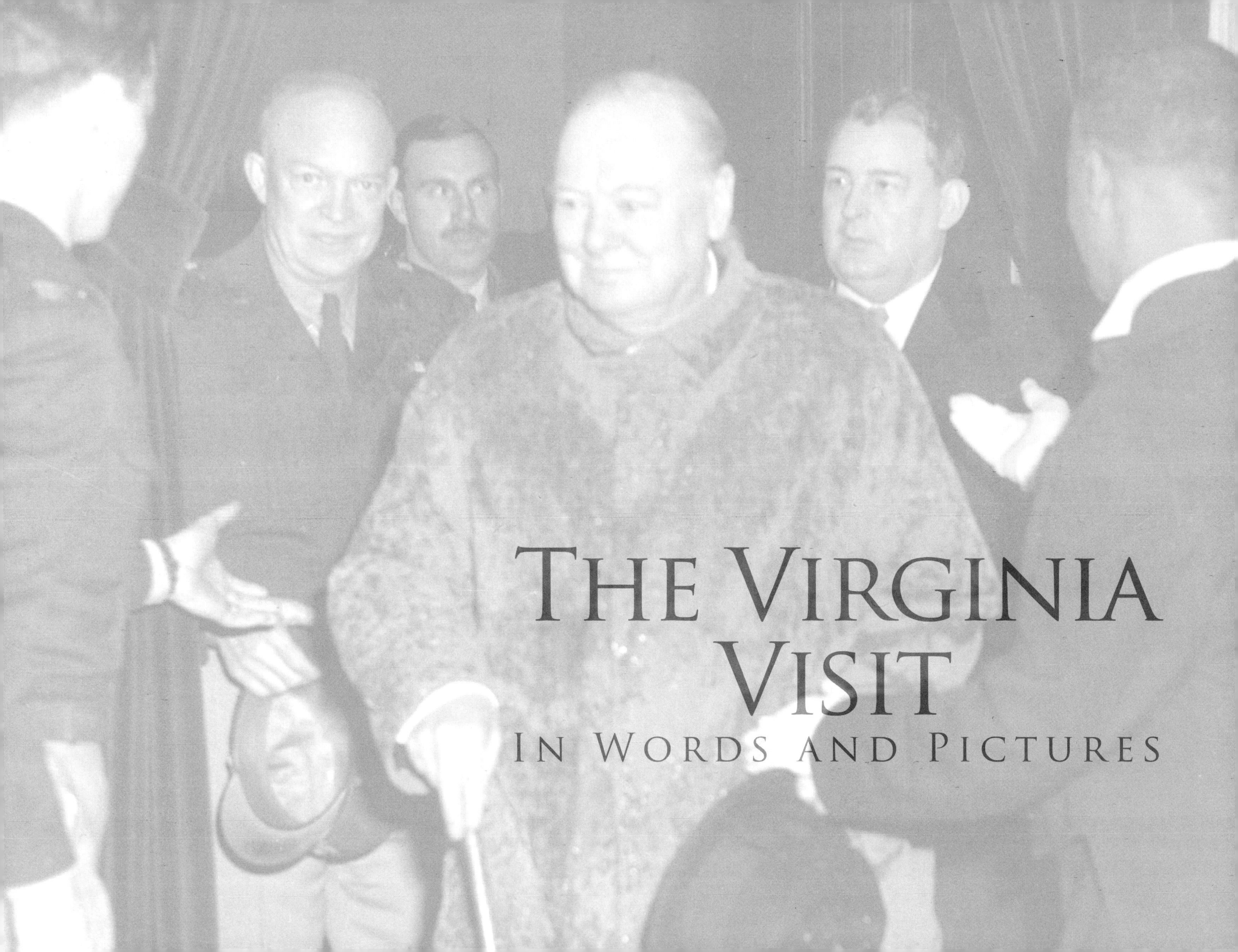

THE VIRGINIA VISIT

IN WORDS AND PICTURES

THE VIRGINIA VISIT: RICHMOND

HOW IT BEGAN

On January 15, 1946, the fifteen-car Havana Special train pulled into Broad Street Station in Richmond, Virginia at 12:09 P.M. Aboard, in a special car, the Springfield, were Winston and Clementine Churchill and their party, which included Churchill's bodyguard, Inspector George Williams of Scotland Yard, his personal physician, Dr. Robert H. Harris, his valet, Mr. Sawyer, Clementine's maid, Miss Miller, and the Churchills' private secretary, Jo Sturdee. They had left Washington, D.C. at 9:30 A.M., en route from New York City, where they had disembarked from the Queen Elizabeth on January 14. Now they were headed to Miami, Florida, for a stay at the home of Colonel Frank Clarke of Quebec. Apparently absorbed in a book or in a conversation with a companion, Mr. Churchill did not even glance out of the window during the twelve minute stopover in Richmond. His secretary informed a reporter that Churchill was "on vacation." But while there was no interview with the famous Englishman, a news photographer did snap a picture of the back of Churchill's head through the train window; it was published in the *Richmond News Leader*[1] along with a brief story. What did happen at the station was that Western Union picked up a Churchill telegram message and was asked to meet the train at several other stops along the southward route.

At the time of the January 15th "sighting," Churchill had only one announced address on his itinerary - a speech at Westminster College in Fulton, Missouri on March 5, 1946. But negotiations may have been underway for other appearances. In a February 13 letter to Governor William Tuck (see Appendix III), Churchill alluded to the fact that conversations with Colonial Williamsburg about a speech there to the Virginia Legislature may have been under discussion early in January, 1946. But it was on January 16, 1946, that Senators John S. Battle and Robert K. Brock introduced a resolution in the Virginia General Assembly formally inviting Churchill to speak to a joint session of the body (in Richmond) at his convenience (see Appendix II). Clerk of the Senate, E. R. Combs, dispatched the adopted resolution, via the British Embassy

---

[1] *Richmond News Leader, January 15, 1946. Churchill as He Arrived in New York.....and as a Few Richmonders Saw Him (picture) p. 1; Churchill, Passing Through , Wouldn't Even Say 'Howdy.' p. 2-B.*

in Washington, to Churchill at the home of Colonel Clarke in Miami Beach, Florida. On February 2, from Cuba, Churchill acknowledged the invitation, but did not commit to an appearance. On the same day (February 2), Governor William Tuck wrote to Churchill through the British Embassy, reiterating the invitation and offering to have Churchill stay in the Governor's Mansion while in Richmond. He stated, *"Because of your inspiration to us and because we would like to prove to you our appreciation for the heroic part you played in the recent international turmoil, I hope that you will see fit to accord us this honor."* [2]

Although Mr. Churchill received speaking requests from the State Legislatures of South Carolina, Kentucky, and Mississippi, he did elect to accept only the Virginia invitation. Confirmation of Mr. Churchill's visit came by way of a private and confidential letter to Governor Tuck on February 13, suggesting March 8, 1946, as the date for Churchill's address, and leaving the details to U. S. British Ambassador, Lord Halifax. Churchill apparently choose March 8 because he had already planned to visit Williamsburg with General Eisenhower on that date (see Churchill's letter of February 13 in Appendix III). That visit to Williamsburg was being negotiated by Bela Norton, a Vice President of Colonial Williamsburg, prior to January 9, 1946, and may have involved a possible address to the Virginia General Assembly convened in special session in Colonial Williamsburg (a suggestion from British Ambassador Lord Halifax). Such sessions were common for the Assembly prior to World War II. [3]
Both P. Solly-Flood at the British Embassy and Captain C. Craig Cannon at the War Office headed by General Dwight Eisenhower, Army Chief of Staff, worked closely with Virginia officials in arranging the Churchill visit. Churchill's original desire to speak to the General Assembly convened in Colonial Williamsburg was rejected on the grounds that there would not be sufficient room for the expected crowd, as well as the fact that the General Assembly would be involved in last-minute wrap-up of their session on March 10. **[Is it possible, had Churchill been accorded the opportunity to speak in historic Williamsburg to what he described as *"the most ancient law-making body on the mainland of the Western Hemisphere,"* [4] that he would have found it appropriate to deliver his "Iron Curtain" speech in Williamsburg instead of at Westminster College in Fulton, Missouri??]**

---

[2] *Letter dated February 2, 1946 from Governor Tuck to Winston Churchill. Governor William M. Tuck Executive Papers (Legislature) 1946, Box 120,* Accession #24026, **The Library of Virginia.**

[3] *Letter dated February 19, 1946 from Governor Tuck to Winston Churchill. Governor William M. Tuck Executive Papers (Legislature) 1946, Box 120,* Accession #24026, **The Library of Virginia.**

[4] *Journal of the Joint Assembly of the General Assembly of the Commonwealth of Virginia, March 8, 1946, House Document No. 25, p. 11.*

On February 17, 1946, it was announced publically that General and Mrs. Dwight Eisenhower and the Earl of Halifax and his wife would accompany Winston Churchill, his wife, Clementine, and daughter, Sarah, when Churchill came to Virginia to address the General Assembly in Richmond on March 8, 1946. (As it turned out, Lord Halifax , because of poor health, was actually unable to make the trip with the Churchills and the Eisenhowers.) Field Marshal Sir Henry Maitland Wilson, accompanied by his aide, Major John Miller, was included in the official party at the behest of the Washington D.C. British Embassy, the suggestion being made in a March 1, 1946 letter [5] from P. Solly-Flood of the embassy staff to Jesse Dillon, secretary to Governor William Tuck. Wilson telegraphed his acceptance on March 6, 1946. [6]

Preparations

With a short turn-around time to prepare for the visit of such illustrious personages, the General Assembly appointed an Arrangements Committee chaired by Delegate E.O. McCue, Jr. and a Reception Committee headed by Governor William Tuck. (See Cast of Characters, p. 38 for a complete list of each committee's membership.) It was decided that the two houses of the General Assembly would convene separately at 10:00 A.M. on March 8, then go into joint session at 10:20 A.M. in the Hall of the House of Delegates. (See floor plan of the Capitol, p. 61.) The vacated Senate chamber would be opened at 10:30 A.M. to a limited number of people from the general public, who could hear the address over loud speakers but not see Churchill in person. The Capitol tunnel system, connecting with other State office buildings would be locked the morning of March 8, to control entrance into the building via that route. All admissions would be through the east entrance into the Capitol.

Capitol Square would be cleared of all but official cars from 4:00 P.M. on March 7 until the departure of the Churchill party around noon on March 8; unauthorized cars would be towed. On March 8, people would be allowed, without tickets, into Capitol Square, where they could witness the arrival and departure of Mr. Churchill through the South Portico. Loud speakers would broadcast the address to those outside the Capitol, and radio broadcasts, carried over local stations WLEE, WMBG, WRNL, and WRVA would make the speech available to countless others around the state and nation. A squadron of twenty-seven State Troopers, under the command of Captain G. M. Williams, was assigned to police the event. They were to be aided by soldiers from Fort Lee and honor guards from the Cadet Corps of Benedictine, John Marshall, and Thomas Jefferson High Schools, who would mark out a corridor through which the official party would enter the Capitol Square.

---

[5] *Letter dated March 1, 1946 from P. Solly-Flood to Jesse Dillon. Governor William M. Tuck Executive Papers (Legislature), 1946. Box 120,* Accession #24026, *The Library of Virginia*

[6] *Telegram of March 6, 1946 from Field Marshal Maitland Wilson. Governor William M. Tuck Executive Papers (Legislature), 1946. Box 120,* Accession #24026, *The Library of Virginia*

With the exception of the 100 Delegates and 40 Senators, who were to be admitted on their own recognizance, admission into the House of Delegates chamber, with a capacity of less than 600, was to be by ticket only. Assembly members were given one ticket apiece for a spouse or other guest. Special guests would include the State's three living former Governors (Senator Harry Byrd, Colgate W. Darden, Jr., and George C. Peery) and their wives; former Speakers of the House of Delegates; members of the Virginia delegation to the U.S. Congress; members of the Virginia Supreme Court of Appeals; heads of the various state departments; Richmond Mayor William Herbert and his wife; Attorney-General Abram Staples and his wife; and the wives of three deceased former Governors, Mrs. John G. Pollard, Mrs. E. Lee Trinkle, and Mrs. Andrew J. Montague. For some reason, it was decided that the Supreme Court of Appeals Justices would be seated in the hall with their backs to the podium and facing the audience during the Churchill address.

To enable thousands of Richmonders to see Winston Churchill and his party, a three-mile parade route was mapped out to carry the motorcade past the statues of some of Virginia's war heroes on the way to the Capitol Building (see map on pp. 58-59). There would be eight automobiles, furnished by Richmond Buick, in the motorcade. A pilot car with Director of Public Safety, James C. Anthony, and Captain C. Craig Cannon, Eisenhower's aide, was to lead the parade. Winston Churchill, General Dwight Eisenhower, Governor William Tuck, and Churchill's Scotland Yard bodyguard, Inspector George Williams, were to occupy the first official car; Lieutenant-Governor Preston Collins would follow in the second car with Mrs. Churchill and Mrs. Eisenhower. The third car would carry Sarah Churchill Oliver, Speaker of the House Thomas Stanley, and Richmond Mayor William Herbert, followed by a car carrying Field Marshal Sir Henry Maitland Wilson, Virginia's Adjutant-General, S. Gardner Waller, Major John Miller, Wilson's aide, and House floor leader, Delegate G. Alvin Massenburg. Following in a fifth car would be Senator Robert Brock, Harold Braham, and Delegate E. Blackburn Moore; then Senator John Battle, Delegate John Spiers, and Mrs. Braham, in a sixth car. In the final car would ride Delegate Stuart Campbell, Charles Campbell of the British Information Services, Senator Robert O. Norris, and Delegate John Daniels. Given good weather the party was to travel in cars with their tops down, but with an ominous prediction from the weatherman for clouds and possible showers on the morning of March 8, contingency plans were for closed cars.

Civic-minded students at John Marshall High School developed a plan to help clean up the city in preparation for the distinguished visitors. Five hundred "Marshalites" signed a letter offering their services in a city-wide clean-up campaign, and a delegation headed by Class President, Kerry Broom, presented the letter to Mayor Herbert on February 27. They also invited like-minded students at Armstrong, Benedictine, Collegiate, Maggie Walker, and Thomas Jefferson High Schools to join in a meeting with Director of Public Works Gamble Bowers, to lay definite plans. It is not clear if this effort really bore fruit. Ultimately, the responsibility of preparing the parade route fell to the Bureau of Street Cleaning, under the direction of Captain John G. Hanna. On March 7, the Department of Public Works went into high gear to clean the streets. Unfortunately, high winds scattered paper and trash, making the job of the street cleaners more difficult. A request from Richmond Police Chief Organ to refrain from parking along the route between 7:00 and 10:00 A.M. on March 7 was largely ignored, perhaps because the police apparently did not post "No Parking" signs. So that afternoon, motorcycle policemen tried to locate owners of cars parked in the way to ask them to move their vehicles. This failing, cars were jacked up to allow employees of the Bureau of Street Cleaning to sweep under them. Public Works Director Bowers exhorted residents along the route to clean up their lawns and put the debris into trash containers rather than throwing it into the streets. At 3 A.M. on March 8, street flushers were used to put the finishing touches on the streets.

Some schools and offices planned to close on the morning of March 8 to allow students and employees to view the parade. At John Marshall High School, Principal Harwood, reversing an earlier ruling on the strength of a petition from 1,000 students, decided to allow the entire student body to attend the parade and speech. Thomas Jefferson High School students were to be allowed to leave school at 9:45 AM and return no later than 11:00 A.M. Other Richmond schools close to the parade route would allow students with a note from home to attend the parade under the supervision of teachers. State offices were to close between 10:00 A.M. and 1:00 P.M.; city employees would be released from 10:00 A.M. until noon. Downtown Richmond's two major department stores, Miller & Rhoads and Thalhimers, announced in the newspapers that they would be closed until 12 noon on Friday, March 8 to allow their employees to witness the parade and participate in other phases of the celebration of Mr. Churchill's and General Eisenhower's visit to the city.

On The Day

Anticipation

In anticipation of the visit of Winston Churchill and Dwight Eisenhower, the Richmond Times Dispatch, on the morning of March 8, 1946, published an editorial which captured the mood and the importance of that day for the citizens of Richmond. The following are excerpts from that editorial: ("*A Great Day in Richmond's Annals,*" Richmond Times Dispatch, p. 16, March 8, 1946)

"Richmond will be host today to two of the supreme figures in world history - Churchill and Eisenhower- men whose names will live for centuries as having stood in the breach when the Axis challenged Western civilization. Without the leadership of Winston Churchill, whose matchless oratory and indomitable courage nerved Britain for its life or death struggle with Hitler, and without the brilliant strategic genius of Eisenhower and his marvelous ability to make men of different nationalities work together, the United States, Britain and the whole of Europe might today be writhing beneath the Nazi heel.

"There has never been a more inspiring personality than Winston Churchill, the very epitome of British greatness as he stood like a granite boulder in the grim days of 1940, when France had fallen and Britain's expeditionary force had staggered back from Dunkirk. It was Churchill, his jaw set and his powerful dynamic figure moving among the ruins of blitzed London or Coventry, which steeled the British for the ordeals which confronted them.

"In a very real sense, then, the British statesman who visits us today saved us here in Virginia, and in America, from invasion by the Axis. For if Britain had gone down when she stood alone against the concentrated might of Nazi Germany, the United States would almost certainly have been attacked simultaneously from the East and West by Germany and Japan, and at a time when we were far from ready.

"One can be equally lyrical concerning the great chief of staff of the United States Army who accompanies Mr. Churchill to Richmond. General Eisenhower is one of those rare spirits whose superlative ability is only matched by his forceful and charming personality. ...... Chosen a few months ago in a poll conducted by a national magazine as the most admired American now living, General Eisenhower is not only the idol of the Army, from buck private to five-star general, but he is the idol of the whole country and of our Allies.

"It will be an occasion never to be forgotten. Those of us who witness it will be able to tell our grandchildren that we saw these shining figures of the Second World War in Richmond on March 8, 1946. Williamsburg, too, will be honored with their presence this afternoon and evening. Thus two Virginia cities whose streets have been trod by many of the country's founding fathers, and whose history is closely interwoven with that of the English-speaking world are fitting hosts today."

Arrival

On March 5, 1946, Winston Churchill, accompanied by President Harry Truman, was in Fulton, Missouri, where Mr. Churchill presented the John Green Lecture, entitled *"Sinews of Peace"*, on the campus of Westminster College. Later known as his "Iron Curtain" speech because of its reference to the growing control by Russia of other countries of Eastern Europe, his address was to ignite widespread controversy both here and abroad and trigger speculation as to whether that controversy would color any of Churchill's subsequent speeches (such as the one to be delivered in Richmond three days later). On March 5, Churchill's wife and daughter were in Washington, D.C. So too was General Dwight D. Eisenhower, serving as Army Chief of Staff. Field Marshal Sir Henry Maitland Wilson, who succeeded Eisenhower as Allied Commander in the Mediterranean during WWII, was in Washington too, assigned as chief of the British Joint Staff Mission. By March 8, Mr. Churchill had returned to Washington aboard the President's train, picked up his family, close war-time friend General Eisenhower and his wife, Mamie, and also Field Marshal Wilson, and was en route, still aboard President Truman's special railroad car, to Richmond, Virginia. British Ambassador Lord Halifax and Lady Halifax did not accompany Churchill, as originally planned, because Lord Halifax was suffering from a relapse of the flu.

For Winston Churchill, General Eisenhower, and their party, the visit to Richmond began very early on March 8, 1946. They reportedly boarded five private cars at the end of the Havana Special at an underground siding in Washington around 1:00 A.M., departing the city at 2:40 A.M. At the controls of locomotive No. 311 was Engineer H. W. Maher. Sixteen journalists, some of them British, occupied one of the five special cars, while military police traveled on another. Mr. Churchill's car was an unnamed Pullman, but General Eisenhower's, the last car on the train, was designated as "One." It was dark when the train rolled into Broad Street Station in Richmond, Virginia at 5:40 A.M., there to be welcomed by Trainmaster Bernard L. Jones, William Tribble, trainer of trainmen, Lucille Coleman, night chief clerk in the station master's office, and Night Chief Dispatcher J. C. Bullock. Initially stopping on track #1 at the far west end of the station, the train would be moved prior to 10 A.M. so that it would be close to cars of the motorcade which would transport the visitors to the Capitol. The train was guarded by a large contingent of military police, commanded by Major E.A. Hutchenson and his assistant Captain J. H. Harrington, and aided by the Richmond police under Captain O.D. Garton.

Members of the official party were sleeping when the train pulled into the station, but lights were already on in the kitchens of the special cars. Everyone was up by 8:30 A.M. Mr. and Mrs. Churchill had breakfast in bed, as did an under-the-weather Mamie Eisenhower, whose light breakfast consisted of grapefruit, toast, and coffee. Churchill's breakfast consisted of grapefruit, eggs, bacon, and coffee. General Eisenhower and Maitland

Wilson ate together. The newspapermen, military police, and others with the group had breakfast at the William Byrd Hotel near the station. (Governor William Tuck had earlier extended an invitation for the Churchill party to breakfast at the Executive Mansion, but it was decided that in the interest of time, it would be more relaxing for the party to eat on the train. Governor Tuck nevertheless hosted a breakfast for other dignitaries including Senator Harry Byrd, and former Governors George Peery and Colgate Darden.)

Before the Reception Committee arrived at 10:00 A.M., Eisenhower was visited on the train by retired Army Lieutenant-Colonel George W. Helms, Eisenhower's commanding officer at Fort Sam Houston immediately after his 1915 graduation from West Point. Colonel Helms had driven from his Roanoke farm expressly to see his "protege," of whom he was justifiably proud. As they chatted for an hour and a half, Eisenhower referred to Helms affectionately as "Ginny," a nickname which Helms was given at West Point because of his Virginia origins. Although it was typically used behind his back by soldiers under his command, Eisenhower had for the first time openly addressed Helms by that nickname in a letter written shortly before the D-Day invasion of France, and it had stuck. As Colonel Helms departed, he neglected to mention that he had no ticket to the General Assembly building, so when Churchill and Eisenhower spoke later that morning, Helms was standing outside in the rain, listening, along with thousands of others, to his friend speak over the P.A. system.

As planned, the Assembly Reception Committee arrived at Broad Street Station at 10:00 A.M. and boarded the train to greet the visiting dignitaries. Members of the party then began to exit the train, to the delight of the huge crowd of station workers, baggage handlers, trainmen, and spectators who had jammed the station's east plaza and balcony overlooking the siding on which the Churchill train had been parked. The first to appear was General Eisenhower, looking trim in a battle jacket and sharply pressed trousers; he was followed by Mamie Eisenhower and Field Marshal Wilson. They were greeted by lights from scores of flashbulbs and by a voice shouting "Hello, Ike," which elicited Ike's famous broad grin and a wave of his hand. Someone handed Mrs. Eisenhower a box which contained an orchid sent by Gray Garland, a Richmonder who had served with Eisenhower in World War I. Eisenhower's aide, Captain C. Craig Cannon helped pin the corsage on Mrs. Eisenhower's black Persian lamb coat, which she wore with a small black straw hat over a light gray suit with a white lace jabot. Her jaunty appearance gave no evidence that, because of some persistent bronchial trouble, it had been uncertain as to whether she would be able to make an appearance in the damp Richmond weather.

OPPOSITE: Governor William M. Tuck (back seat center), chairman of the Reception Committee, with Winston Churchill (left) and General Dwight Eisenhower (right) leaves the Broad Street Train Station in a Buick furnished for the occasion by Richmond Buick. Churchill, sporting his trademark cigar and famous "V for victory" hand sign, elects to ride with the top down despite a persistent and sometimes drenching rain. Next to the driver, but not seen in this picture, is Churchill's Scotland Yard bodyguard, Inspector George E. Williams.

(Unfortunately the weatherman's forecast of clouds and rain for the morning of March 8, had come true. Rain, heavy at times, was to follow the party along the motorcade route to the Capitol.)

Next to alight from the train to the applause of the assembled crowd were Clementine Churchill and Sarah Churchill Oliver. Mrs. Churchill wore a navy felt hat and a navy blue suit with a red camellia in the lapel, a gift from the Richmond chapter of the English-Speaking Union presented to her on the train by Mrs. Thomas Duffy. Red-haired Sarah , the second of Churchill's daughters, wore a black outfit and a small black hat with a chartreuse flower on the right side. Once married to orchestra leader Vic Oliver, she had served in the Women's Auxiliary Air Force during the war as an interpretive officer and had accompanied her father to the Casablanca and Yalta conferences as his secretary.

Note: At this point Richmond photographer Frank Dementi began his coverage of the Richmond - Williamsburg visit. He was to follow the party all the way until midnight. All the photographs of the day in the rest of this narrative are printed from his original negatives.

As Winston Churchill emerged from the train, the crowd, waiting patiently in the rain, broke into a roar of applause, cheers and whistles. Churchill, in a brown, nondescript raincoat, paused on the observation platform of his special car, puffing away on his big cigar. He grinned, doffed his hat to the crowd and waved with his famous "V-for-victory" sign. Then, sticking his cigar back into his mouth, he stepped to the ground, posed for photographs, and proceeded to the waiting automobiles. Despite the rain, he elected to ride in the parade motorcade with the car top down. He stepped into the first of the official cars. Crammed into the back seat along with General Eisenhower and Governor Tuck, and with bodyguard Inspector Williams in the front passenger seat, Churchill was off along a wet three-mile-long parade route to the State Capitol. (See map pp. 58-59) Leaving Broad Street Train Station (now the Science Museum of Virginia), the motorcade first traveled west on Broad Street to the Boulevard, south on the Boulevard to Monument Avenue, then east on Monument Avenue and its continuation, Franklin Street, passing by the statues of Stonewall Jackson, Jefferson Davis, Robert E. Lee, and J.E.B. Stuart. At First and Franklin Streets, photographer Frank Dementi snapped a picture of the car carrying Winston Churchill, Governor Tuck, and General Eisenhower. Arriving in downtown Richmond, the

---

OPPOSITE: In this photograph, the first official car in the eight car motorcade passes the corner of what has been identified as First and Franklin Streets. During the course of the three mile trip to the Capitol, Winston Churchill rides atop the back seat of the open car, frequently giving his "victory" hand sign. Here the sign is returned by an on-looker on the corner. Seated on the left side of the car, General Dwight Eisenhower flashes his famous smile and waves to the crowd. It was estimated by the Virginia Historical Society that 30,000 people stood in the rain along the parade route to welcome the former British Prime Minister and General Eisenhower.

Route of the Churchill Motorcade Through Richmond

This map shows the route which was taken by the Churchill motorcade after leaving Richmond's Broad Street Train Station (now the Science Museum of Virginia). The eight cars traveled west on Broad Street from the station, turned south onto the Boulevard, then east along Monument Avenue, past the statues of Stonewall Jackson, Jefferson Davis, Robert E. Lee, and J.E.B. Stuart, and onto Franklin Street, a continuation of Monument Avenue. Photographer Frank Dementi captured a picture of the motorcade as it passed First and Franklin Streets. (See p. 57.) Arriving in downtown Richmond, the motorcade turned north onto Fifth Street, then east onto Grace Street. It entered the grounds of Capitol Square at Ninth and Grace, and circled right around the Capitol building to discharge passengers in front of the South Portico steps. The map includes pictures of the following relevant Richmond locations mentioned in the accompanying narrative:

1. *Broad Street Station - 2500 West Broad Street*
2. *St. James Episcopal Church - 1205 West Franklin Street*
3. *Hillyard-Maury House on the southwest corner of First and Franklin Streets*
4. *Virginia State Capitol in Capitol Square - Ninth and Grace Streets*
5. *Main Street Station - East Main Street at Fifteenth Street*

The three area high schools whose cadet corps formed an honor guard for the motorcade:

6. *Thomas Jefferson High School - West Grace Street at Malvern Avenue*
7. *Benedictine High School - 304 North Sheppard Street*
8. *John Marshall High School - Marshall Street at Eighth Street*

It also indicates the location of the Confederate War statues passed by the Churchill motorcade:

- A *Stonewall Jackson on Monument Avenue at the Boulevard*
- B *Jefferson Davis on Monument Avenue at North Davis Street*
- C *Robert E. Lee on Monument Avenue at Allen Avenue*
- D *J.E.B. Stuart on Monument Avenue at Lombardy*

Map courtesy of the Greater Richmond Chamber of Commerce through the Virginia Historical Society

1
2
3
4
5
6
7
8
A
B
C
D
N
S
E
W
BROAD
GRACE
FRANKLIN
MAIN
CARY
MONUMENT AVE
BOULEVARD
BROAD ST STATION
CAPITOL SQUARE
RIVER
JAMES
SETTLING BASIN

motorcade turned north onto Fifth Street, then east onto Grace Street to Ninth Street. Armed soldiers from Camp Lee in Petersburg, uniformed city police, and State Troopers were stationed at every intersection along the parade route to maintain order; the Camp Lee soldiers were members of Headquarters Company, Company A, and Company B of the Demonstration Batallion. Entering Capitol Square at Ninth and Grace Streets, the cars passed the equestrian statue of George Washington, circled to the right around the Capitol Building, and discharged their passengers at the foot of the South Portico steps.

An estimated crowd of 30,000 umbrella-toting men, women, and children packed the parade route on both sides of the street. Many had been standing in drizzling rain since before 9:00 A.M. One rain-soaked woman remarked, *"We're providing home-like weather for our visitors from London."* [7] Soon after leaving Broad Street Station, Mr. Churchill voluntarily climbed onto the back of the seat, where he rode, bare-headed, giving his famous victory salute. Occasionally he would replace his hat as protection against the rain, but it would soon come off again. The crowds cheered, sometimes returning Churchill's victory sign. At times, an onlooker would shout "Hello Ike" and be rewarded with a snappy salute and Eisenhower's famous grin. Confetti often rained down in addition to Nature's raindrops. (At one point a bag of confetti dropped into Churchill's vehicle and exploded.) Thousands of school children lining the parade route waved British and American flags. Doctors, nurses, and patients at hospitals along the route jammed balconies to see the procession. As the parade passed St. James Episcopal Church on Franklin Street, its bells tolled "God Save the King." In the downtown district, crowds surging into the streets threatened to block passage of the cars.

[7] *Justices Face Hard Decision On Which Churchill To Face, Richmond News Leader, March 8, 1946, p. 15.*

This photograph of the Virginia State Capitol, taken by Frank Dementi around 1925 from the top of the Rueger Hotel at Ninth and Bank Streets, clearly shows the South Portico steps which Churchill and Eisenhower ascended to enter the building. The motorcade would have entered the Capitol grounds via the road which circles to the right, past the equestrian statue of George Washington Ⓐ*, around and to the front of the portico steps.* Ⓑ *On March 8, 1946, as the motorcade passed through, this pathway was lined by the honor guard of cadets from Benedictine, John Marshall, and Thomas Jefferson High Schools. Behind and to the left of the Capitol (in the picture) is the Richmond City Hall.*

As the motorcade neared the Capitol grounds, from Eighth Street to the South Portico of the Capitol, it passed between lines of rain-soaked honor guard cadets from Benedictine, John Marshall, and Thomas Jefferson High Schools, all standing at rigid attention. It was later reported by Charles Campbell, director of the British Information Services, that Mr. Churchill had been very much impressed by the smart military appearance of the cadets and wished his compliments on their excellent bearing to be conveyed to them. In a letter to Colonel Earl Brown, Commandant of the John Marshall Corps, General Eisenhower likewise conveyed a similar message (see letter, p. 122). Cadets from Thomas Jefferson High School broke ranks before Churchill had completed his visit to the General Assembly, allowing them to change their rain-soaked clothing and return to afternoon classes. On the other hand, members of the John Marshall Cadet Band, who had followed the motorcade to the South Portico steps, held ranks while they listened to Churchill's speech. When the party left the Capitol, those cadets were on hand to present arms.

Arriving at the South Portico of the Capitol, Churchill, Eisenhower, and Governor Tuck, followed by their entourage, mounted the steps in a drenching rain and stood at attention as the Marine Band from Quantico, Virginia, played the national anthems of the United States and Great Britain. They then proceeded into the building, past the historic Houdon statue of George Washington in the Rotunda and into the former Hall of the House of Delegates with its striking Evans statue of General Robert E. Lee (See pictures, p. 65.). Here the visitors and Reception Committee members shed their wraps and mingled briefly. Churchill and Eisenhower posed for pictures as if they were signing the official guest register, but before the act was actually accomplished, General Eisenhower noticed the non-smoking signs in the room and hastened outside to douse his lit cigarette. In the confusion afterwards, the book never got signed, although it was erroneously reported later that an autograph seeker had made away with the signed page. It was also during this time in the old Hall of the House of Delegates, that, we believe, Clementine Churchill, who had been photographed by Frank Dementi on a previous visit to Colonial Williamsburg, Virginia (September 8, 1943), advised him to be present at the Raleigh Tavern in Williamsburg at 5:00 P.M. that afternoon.

(Story continued on page 74.)

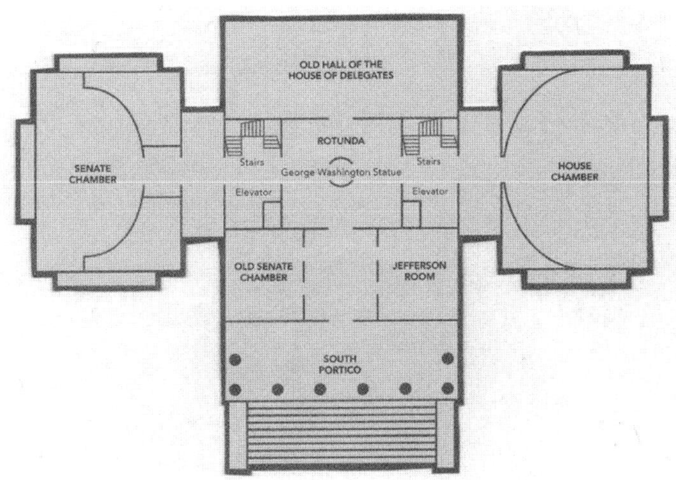

Diagram of the first floor of the State Capitol, showing the South Portico, the Rotunda, and the Old Hall of the House of Delegates. Churchill's speech was delivered in the House Chamber (east wing). Courtesy of the Virginia State Capitol.

General Dwight Eisenhower, Winston Churchill, and Virginia Governor William Tuck (L to R) ascend the steps of the South Portico of the Virginia State Capitol. Evidence of the morning rain can be seen on Eisenhower's uniform, Churchill's coat, and the glistening wet steps. At the base of the steps, some of the honor guard of high school cadets can be seen standing at attention in the rain. Unlike the cadets, some people in the assembled crowd stand protected under umbrellas.

As Winston Churchill, General Eisenhower, and Governor Tuck reach the South Portico, the Quantico Marine Band plays "God Save the King" and "The Star Spangled Banner." Eisenhower's salute would suggest that the United States anthem is being played at the time this picture was snapped.

OPPOSITE: A rain-spattered Churchill (center) is welcomed as he enters the old Hall of the House of Delegates. Behind him to the left is General Dwight Eisenhower and to the right is Governor William Tuck. Behind Eisenhower, is Chief Inspector George Williams, Churchill's Scotland Yard bodyguard. Greeting the party are two Capitol workers. The young man in uniform on the left may be twenty-one-year old William E. Daniel of Charlotte Court House, an ex GI, now House Page, who had been posted near the door. The gentleman to Churchill's left may be Tom Bannister, a veteran butler at the Executive Mansion. In the right foreground is a portion of the Evans statue of General Robert E. Lee, which stands in the hall just inside the entrance.

LEFT: This statue of General Robert E. Lee stands just inside the old Hall of the House of Delegates at the Virginia Capitol, on the very site where Lee accepted command of the Armed Forces of Virginia on April 23, 1861. Sculpted by Rudulph Evans and cast in New York State in 1931, it was unveiled in Richmond, Virginia, on January 19, 1932. Photographer Frank Dementi took this picture probably at or near the time of the unveiling. Behind the Lee statue in the photograph is the cast iron railing which surrounds the Jean-Antoine Houdon statue of George Washington, located in the Capitol Rotunda.

BELOW: This marble statue of George Washington in the rotunda of the Virginia State Capitol stands a life-sized six feet two inches high. Sculpted by Jean-Antoine Houdon, who visited Mount Vernon in 1785 to make sketches and a plaster cast of Washington's face, the sculpture is considered a perfect likeness.
Photo by Frank Dementi

The old Hall of the House of Delegates in the Virginia State Capitol, which served as a gathering place for the Churchill entourage on March 8, 1946, was the meeting chamber for the Virginia House of Delegates from 1788 until 1904. Two wings, completed in 1906, then provided new meeting rooms for both the Senate and the House of Delegates. Between 1904 and 1946, the old Hall was used for official business only once. A Constitutional Convention met there on October 25, 1933, to consider and approve the amendment repealing Prohibition. (Virginia thus became the thirty-second state to ratify the Constitutional amendment.) Frank Dementi was present at that meeting and recorded the event in this photograph. The picture serves well to show details of the room, notably the location of the General Robert E. Lee statue (at the left side of the picture) and the ornate balcony/gallery.

Waiting for the joint session of the General Assembly to begin, members of the Churchill party and the Reception Committee mingle in the old Hall of the House of Delegates. Churchill and Eisenhower pose to sign the official guest register. In this picture Winston Churchill, Governor William Tuck, and General Dwight Eisenhower (L to R) chat. Behind and to Eisenhower's left is Lieutenant-Governor L. Preston Collins. The gentleman in glasses facing right between Churchill and Tuck may be Delegate E. Blackburn Moore from Berryville, Virginia, a member of the Reception Committee. The gentleman over Churchill's right shoulder is thought to be Harold Braham, British Consul in Baltimore.

Prior to the joint session of the Virginia General Assembly, General Dwight Eisenhower engages in conversation in the old Hall of the House of Delegates with a member of the Reception Committee, Speaker of the House, Thomas Stanley. The gentleman in the background is probably Mr. Harold Braham, British Consul in Baltimore.

Clementine Churchill, wife of Winston Churchill, stands in the Rotunda just outside the entrance to the old Hall of the House of Delegates with her escort, Delegate Edward McCue. She will be introduced to the Assembly and seated in the second row of the House Chamber prior to Churchill's speech. The Robert E. Lee statue is visible behind her. It may have been at this time that she instructed her photographer, Frank Dementi, to be sure to be at the Raleigh Tavern in Colonial Williamsburg at 5:00 PM that afternoon.

General Dwight Eisenhower stands at the entrance to the old Hall of the House of Delegates with his escort, Senator Robert O. Norris, Jr. (on his left), awaiting introduction to the joint session of the Virginia General Assembly in the House Chamber of the Capitol. The Robert E. Lee statue is seen behind him. The gentleman at the left is unidentified.

Winston Churchill stands at the entrance to the House Chamber of the Virginia State Capitol. He is escorted by Senator Robert Kincaid Brock (on his left) and introduced to the joint session by Sergeant-at-Arms, Dr. Lovick P. Law (not in the picture). He is saluted here by two unidentified state policemen as he enters. The gentleman behind Churchill is also unidentified.

"The strife is o'er, the battle won." A relaxed Winston Churchill (left) and General Dwight Eisenhower (center) are caught on camera by photographer Frank Dementi prior to the beginning of the joint session of the Virginia General Assembly. Seated to Eisenhower's left is Senate Clerk E.R. Combs. Behind the trio, on the House Speaker's platform, are Governor William Tuck, House Speaker Thomas Stanley, and Lieutenant-Governor L. Preston Collins (L to R).

After being introduced to the joint session of the Virginia General Assembly, Field Marshal Sir Henry Maitland Wilson, Winston Churchill and General Dwight Eisenhower (L to R) are seated at the front of the hall just below the House Speaker's platform. Here they pose briefly for photographer Frank Dementi before the session officially begins.

Address

At 10:20 A.M., the Senate followed its clerk, E. R. Combs, into the Hall of the House of Delegates to join the assembled delegates. Roll calls certified that there were 38 of 40 Senators present and 97 of 100 Delegates present. The five World War II veterans who were members of the House of Delegates were present, impressive in their uniforms. These included Captain G. Alvin Massenburg, Coast Guard; Lieutenant-Commander Walter H. Scott, USNR; Major Shelton H. Short, Jr., USMC; Captain Virgil H. Goode, AUS; and Lieutenant William J. Gibson, Army Air Forces. Senator Edward L. Breeden, Jr., and Delegates Edmund T. DeJarnette and William R. Shaffer, were appointed to inform Governor William Tuck that the Joint Assembly was in session and to invite him to be present. Then the following distinguished guests were presented and seated in the closely-packed chamber:

1. Former Speakers of the House, Messrs. Cardwell, Houston, Brown, and Dovell
2. Six of the nine Virginia members of the U.S. House of Representatives - S. Otis Bland (First District), Ralph H. Daughton (Second District), J. Vaughan Gary (Third District), Patrick H. Drewry (Fourth District), T. G. Burch (Fifth District), and A. Willis Robertson [8] (Seventh District)
3. Justices of the Virginia Supreme Court of Appeals, and Attorney General Abram Staples
4. Former Governors of the Commonwealth of Virginia, Harry Byrd, George Peery, and Colgate Darden

After this, House Speaker Thomas Stanley, and President of the Senate (also Lieutenant Governor) L. Preston Collins entered the hall together and took their places on the speaker's platform.

Beginning at 10:55 A.M., members of the Churchill entourage were announced to the joint session by Sergeant-at-Arms Dr. Lovick P. Law and escorted into the chamber by members of the Arrangements and Reception Committees. First came Governor Tuck, followed by Richmond Mayor Herbert, Mrs. Churchill (escorted by Delegate Edward McCue), Mrs. Eisenhower (escorted by Senator Harry Stuart), Mrs. Sarah Oliver (escorted by Delegate John Warren Cooke), Mrs. Harold Braham, wife of the British Consul at Baltimore (escorted by Delegate G. Edmond Massie), Harold

[8] *A guest of Representative A. Willis Robertson was Commander Raymond Guest, USNR, a first cousin once removed of Winston Churchill, who with Representative Robertson, had recently visited Churchill in Florida.*

At 11:02 AM Winston Churchill begins his twenty minute address to the joint session of the Virginia General Assembly. Here he can be seen delivering his speech. He is flanked to the left by Field Marshal Sir Henry Maitland Wilson and to the right by General Dwight Eisenhower. Behind him are (L to R) Governor William Tuck, House Speaker Thomas Stanley, Lieutenant-Governor L. Preston Collins, and Delegate Edward McCue, Chairman of the Arrangements Committee. The address is carried by the four local Richmond radio stations, WLEE, WMBG, WRNL, and WRVA, whose microphones are visible at the podium.

At the conclusion of his address, Winston Churchill receives a standing ovation from the audience. In this picture he stands at the podium with Field Marshal Wilson to his right and General Eisenhower to his left. Behind them between the flags are (L to R) Governor William Tuck, Speaker of the House, Thomas Stanley, and Lieutenant Governor L. Preston Collins. The Justices of the Virginia Supreme Court are in the first row of the audience. In the second row, to the left of the aisle stand {R to L), Clementine Churchill, Mrs. William Tuck, Mamie Eisenhower, and Sarah Churchill Oliver. A more complete identification of members of the audience is provided on pp. 42-43.

Braham, and James Guthrie. Then Field Marshal Sir Henry Maitland Wilson drew heavy applause as he was seated. While waiting his turn to enter the General Assembly, General Eisenhower spotted the lapel shield of the Fifteenth Infantry Regiment on the left shoulder of the uniform of ex-GI, now House Page, William E. Daniel, Jr., 21, of Charlotte Court House, who was posted near the door. After a quick handshake, Ike entered into a brief conversation with Ex-Technician Fifth Grade Daniel. When it was Eisenhower's turn to be introduced, the crowd went wild as the former Supreme Allied Commander, presented by Senator Robert O. Norris, Jr., came down the aisle, grinning broadly. Then after a dramatic pause, the Sergeant-at-Arms announced, *"Mr. Speaker, the Right Honorable Winston Spencer Churchill,"* and to the accompaniment of whistles, cheers, and vigorous hand-clapping, the Briton, presented by Senator Robert K. Brock, strolled in leisurely fashion down the aisle, bowed slightly, shook a few hands, and took his seat near the rostrum between Field Marshal Wilson and General Eisenhower. Reception committee members also presented Major Miller, Captain Craig Cannon, and Inspector George Williams, who were formally received by the Assembly. The wives and other members of the Churchill party sat in the second row of the audience.

At 11:01 Speaker Stanley introduced Mr. Churchill, as *"a member of Parliament and the leader of the Conservative Party in the House of Commons - Britain's wartime Prime Minister - leader for the Allied nations during the years of battle."* [9] Churchill then began his twenty-minute address to the General Assembly at 11:02 A.M. Departing from his prepared text on several occasions,[10] Winston Churchill at one point gave praise to General Eisenhower, citing his *"single-hearted purpose, his wide and profound views on military science, and his great power of making soldiers, officers, and men of our two countries work together under all the shocks and strains of war as though they were soldiers of one single nation."* This unity of purpose and cooperation of the two English-speaking nations was a recurrent theme in his speech. As Churchill concluded, there was again thunderous applause, then an expectant hush. Calls for Eisenhower began, causing the General to rise, bow, and flash his grin. Before he could sit down, cries of "Speech, speech," resounded. After being presented by Speaker Thomas Stanley, Ike responded with a brief tribute to Churchill, asserting that *"Of all the things that supported me through three and a half years of warfare on the European continent, I know of no other single thing that was of greater moral benefit than the unwavering, staunch, indomitable, courageous support of the Prime Minister of Great Britain."* (See Appendix IV for full text of the Churchill and Eisenhower speeches.)

---

[9] *Journal of the Joint Assembly of the General Assembly of the Commonwealth of Virginia. March 8, 1946, House Document No. 25, p. 10.*

[10] *At one point in his address, Churchill made allusion to the fact the Douglas Southall Freeman, Pulitzer-Prize-winning Richmond author, was in the audience.*

RIGHT: In a brief speech, General Dwight Eisenhower addresses the Virginia General Assembly, lauding Churchill and making reference to his own Virginia roots through his mother. In this picture, Eisenhower is at the podium. He is flanked by Field Marshal Sir Henry Maitland Wilson to his right and Winston Churchill and Senate Clerk Combs to his left. Governor William Tuck (L) and Lieutenant Governor L. Preston Collins (R) sit at the House Speaker's platform, but House Speaker Thomas Stanley (center) cannot be seen. To Collins' left in front of the flag is Delegate Edward McCue. The six gentlemen seated in front of the podium and turning around to look at Eisenhower are Justices of the Virginia Supreme Court of Appeals.

BELOW: After calls for General Eisenhower to speak following Winston Churchill's address, House Speaker Thomas Stanley (standing) simply announces, "General Eisenhower," and Eisenhower (at the podium) delivers a brief extemporaneous speech.

NBC
WMBG
WRNL
American Broadcasting Company

After the speeches, the distinguished visitors were escorted out of the House Chamber, and the Joint Assembly was declared adjourned. As Churchill entered the corridor, a ripple of applause from men and women crowded on the steps leading down from the gallery elicited the familiar V-for-victory salute. Just as the party was exiting the Capitol, an unidentified spectator passed a bottle of champagne through the cordon of police and plainclothes police guards. It was iced down in a silver bucket and was accompanied by an unsigned note praising Churchill as a hero and requesting that the bucket be returned to the Mayor's office. The champagne was placed in Churchill's automobile and presumably transferred to the waiting train; the bucket was returned by that afternoon. As Churchill stepped out onto the South Portico to the cheers of people who had been waiting two hours in the rain to catch a glimpse of the British statesman, he stopped for a moment and again raised his right hand in the victory salute. Then he descended, in company with General Eisenhower and former Governor Colgate Darden, to a car waiting to carry them to Main Street Train Station for a trip to Colonial Williamsburg. Following them in a second car were Mrs. Churchill and Mrs. Darden. A last car carried Field Marshal Wilson. On arrival at Main Street Station, Mr. Churchill boarded the train immediately, apparently because he was hungry and ready for lunch. An obliging General Eisenhower, however, stood alone on the rear platform of the train, grinning and saluting in farewell to another large crowd as the train pulled out into the soggy mist.

OPPOSITE: At the conclusion of the joint session of the Virginia General Assembly, Winston Churchill and General Dwight Eisenhower depart from the State Capitol in the company of former Virginia Governor Colgate Darden. In this photograph, Churchill and Eisenhower sit in their car (here with the top raised) waiting to depart for Main Street Station, where they will board the train for a one hour trip to Colonial Williamsburg, Virginia. Seated in the front seat again is Churchill's bodyguard, Inspector George Williams of Scotland Yard. A careful look at the background shows at top left a bit of the Richmond Hotel, located at the northwest corner of Ninth and Grace Streets. On the steps of the Capitol stand some of the crowd that had been waiting in the rain to bid farewell to their heroes.

S.M.B.

THE VIRGINIA VISIT : WILLIAMSBURG

ARRIVAL

The special train carrying the Churchill party departed Main Street Station in Richmond, Virginia at noon on March 8, 1946, arrived in Williamsburg at 1:16 P.M., and parked on a railroad siding behind the Governor's Palace, where the party lunched on the train. General Eisenhower had remarked on leaving Richmond in the rain, that he *"would give a farm"* [11] for the sun to be shining in Williamsburg. He got his wish. The sun came out as the party was arriving and stayed out for the better part of the afternoon. Leaving the other members of the party to rest and change, Eisenhower, along with former Governor Colgate Darden and Field Marshal Sir Henry Maitland Wilson, slipped away undetected after lunch and motored seven miles to tour historic Jamestown, home of the first permanent English settlement in the New World (1607). [Making this trip was consistent with Eisenhower's reported interest in history, which may have been one of the factors considered by President Franklin Roosevelt in choosing Eisenhower to be Supreme Allied Commander for Operation Overlord (the D-Day invasion of the French beaches of Normandy)]. Returning to Williamsburg, Eisenhower, Wilson, and Darden joined the rest of the party to emerge from the train shortly before 3:30 P.M. As they stepped off the train onto mats laid over the muddy ground, they were greeted by the town fathers (including Mayor Channing Hall, City Councilmen Dr. H. M. Stryker, Lloyd H. Williams, John G. Warburton, Vincent D. McManus, and City Manager W. R. Woodbury), along with some officials of Colonial Williamsburg Foundation, Inc. An estimated 5,000 residents were also on hand, so excited that they often broke through cordons of local police trying to control contact with the visitors. Churchill, thinking he recognized a familiar face, struck up a conversation with a surprised Richmond photographer, Joe Colognori, who assured Mr. Churchill that they had never met.

---

[11] *Assembly sidelights. Richmond News Leader, March 11, 1946. p 5.*

OPPOSITE: The Churchill train arrived in Colonial Williamsburg at 1:16 PM and parked on a siding behind the Governor's Palace. But it was not until 3:30 PM, after lunch and a rest period, that members of the party emerged from the train to be greeted by the Williamsburg Welcoming Committee, headed by Mayor Channing Hall. In this picture, General Eisenhower (left) and Winston Churchill (right) are the first to leave the train, followed by Churchill's wife, Clementine (who has changed her hat since leaving Richmond). Next to exit will be Mamie Eisenhower, followed by Mrs. Colgate Darden. The train conductor is unidentified. Again Churchill is sporting his trademark cigar.

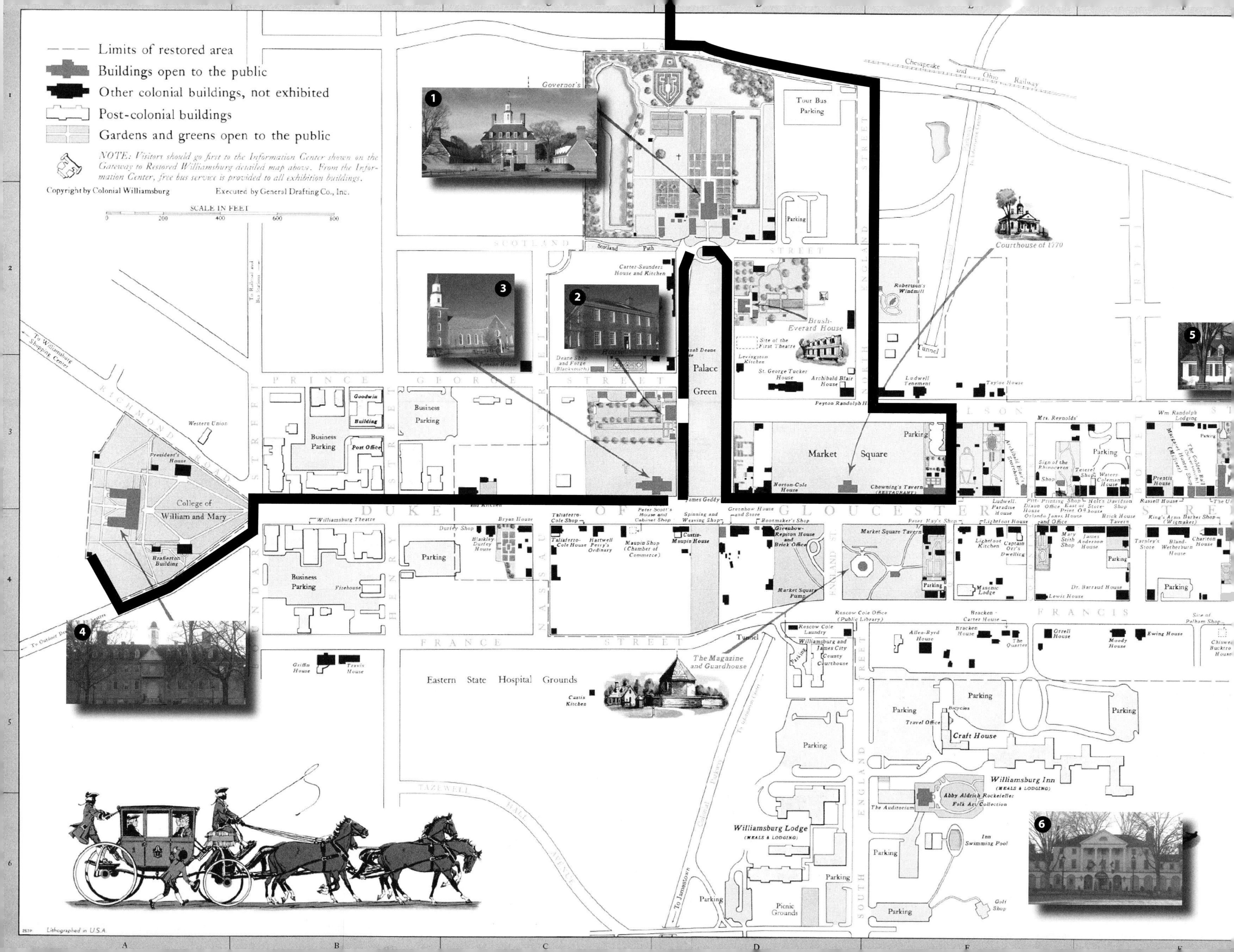

Limits of restored area
Buildings open to the public
Other colonial buildings, not exhibited
Post-colonial buildings
Gardens and greens open to the public
NOTE: Visitors should go first to the Information Center shown on the Gateway to Restored Williamsburg detailed map above. From the Information Center, free bus service is provided to all exhibition buildings.
Copyright by Colonial Williamsburg
Executed by General Drafting Co., Inc.
SCALE IN FEET
0
200
400
600
800
1
2
3
4
5
6
Chesapeake and Ohio Railway
Tour Bus Parking
Parking
Scotland Path
SCOTLAND
STREET
NORTH ENGLAND STREET
Courthouse of 1770
Carter-Saunders House and Kitchen
Robertson's Windmill
Brush-Everard House
Site of the First Theatre
Levingston Kitchen
St. George Tucker House
Archibald Blair House
Peyton Randolph H
Ludwell Tenement
Tayloe House
Tunnel
Palace Green
PRINCE
GEORGE
Goodwin
Building
Business Parking
Post Office
Western Union
RICHMOND ROAD
To Williamsburg Shopping Center
President's House
College of William and Mary
Brafferton Building
Market Square
Norton-Cole House
Chowning's Tavern (RESTAURANT)
Mrs. Reynolds'
Wm Randolph Lodging
Sign of the Rhinoceros
Prentis House
Ludwell-Paradise House
Russell House
James Geddy
Greenhow House and Store
Bootmaker's Shop
Williamsburg Theatre
Bryan House
Taliaferro-Cole Shop
Peter Scott's House and Cabinet Shop
Spinning and Weaving Shop
Durfey Shop
Blaikley Durfey House
Taliaferro-Cole House
Hartwell Perry's Ordinary
Maupin Shop (Chamber of Commerce)
Custis-Maupin House
Greenhow-Repiton House and Brick Office
Market Square Tavern
Peter Hay's Shop
Lightfoot House
Lightfoot Kitchen
Captain Orr's Dwelling
Masonic Lodge
Mary Stith Shop
James Anderson House
Brick House Tavern
King's Arms Barber Shop (Wigmaker)
Tarpley's Store
Bland-Wetherburn House
Chiswell House
Dr. Barraud House
Lewis House
Market Square Pump
DUKE OF GLOUCESTER
Parking
Firehouse
FRANCE
STREET
FRANCIS
Roscow Cole Office (Public Library)
Bracken-Carter House
Roscow Cole Laundry
Williamsburg and James City County Courthouse
Allen-Byrd House
Bracken House
The Quarter
Orrell House
Moody House
Ewing House
Site of Pelham Shop
Griffin House
Travis House
Eastern State Hospital Grounds
Custis Kitchen
The Magazine and Guardhouse
Tunnel
Colonial Parkway
To Jamestown
Bicycles
Travel Office
Craft House
Williamsburg Inn (MEALS & LODGING)
Abby Aldrich Rockefeller Folk Art Collection
The Auditorium
Inn Swimming Pool
Williamsburg Lodge (MEALS & LODGING)
Picnic Grounds
Golf Shop
SOUTH ENGLAND STREET
TAZEWELL HALL AVENUE
Lithographed in U.S.A.
A
B
C
D
E
F

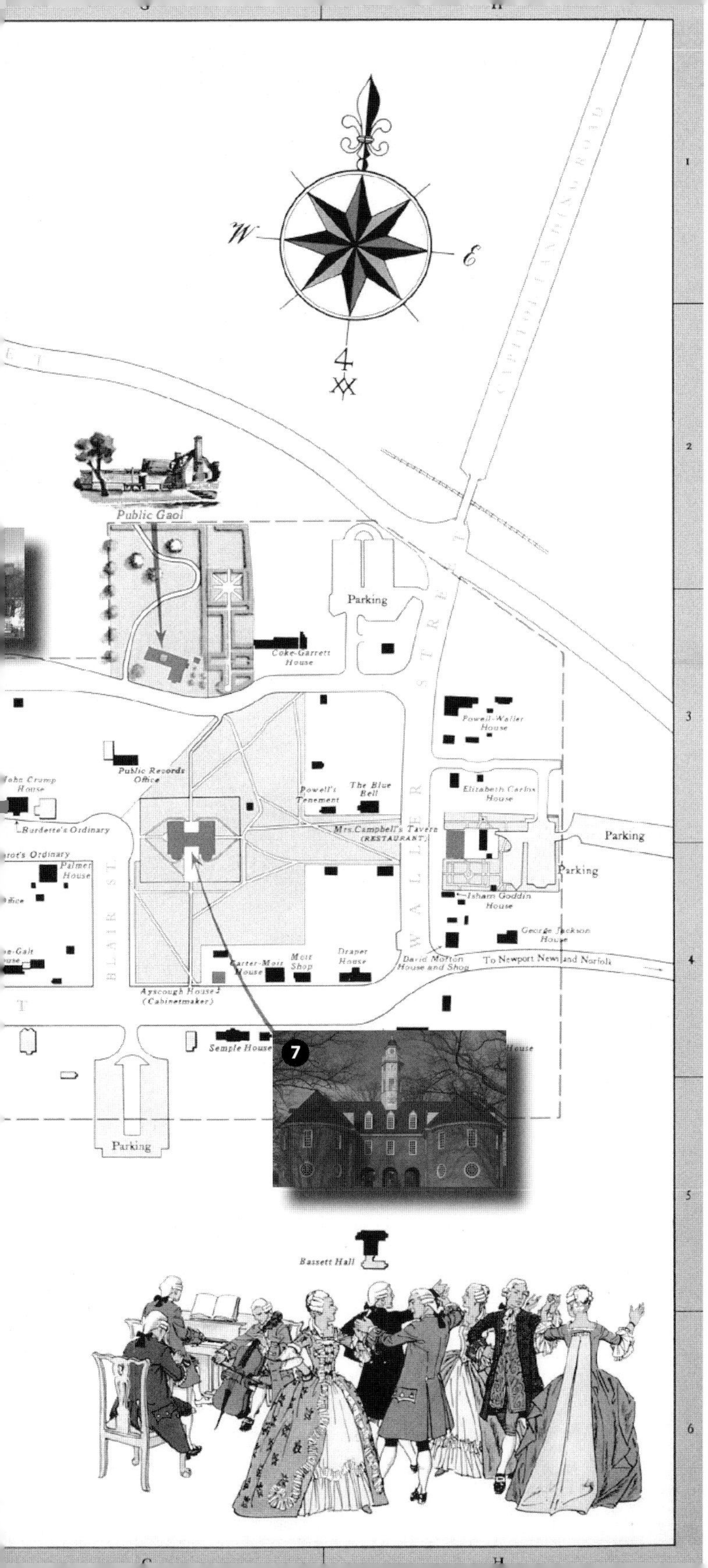

Route of the Churchill Party Through Colonial Williamsburg

Leaving the train siding at the rear of the Governor's Palace, the Churchill entourage motored east on Lafayette Street, turned right onto North England Street, then left onto Nicholson, right onto Queen Street, right onto Duke of Gloucester Street, and finally right onto Palace Green Street, which leads to the front of the Governor's Palace. The original plan was for the dignitaries, after touring the Governor's Palace, to leave in horse-drawn coaches, which would take them east on Duke of Gloucester Street, pausing for photographs at the Capitol, then returning back down Duke of Gloucester Street to Bruton Parish Church. After a brief tour of the church, they would use cars to travel to the College of William and Mary at the west end of Duke of Gloucester Street, then back up the street to the Raleigh Tavern, and finally to the Williamsburg Inn off of Francis Street. Problems with the horses forced the abandonment of the coach rides at the Palace, causing the party to walk from the Palace to the George Wythe House on the Palace Green, then walk to Bruton Parish Church. Here they picked up the cars as originally planned, to drive west along Duke of Gloucester Street to the College of William and Mary and tour the Christopher Wren Building. From there, they motored back east on Duke of Gloucester Street for a quick look at the Capitol, which they would tour after dinner. Then it was on to the Raleigh Tavern for a reception hosted by Kenneth Chorley, President of Colonial Williamsburg and his wife, Jean. They ended up at the Williamsburg Inn for an elegant dinner hosted by Mr. and Mrs. John D. Rockefeller, III. After dinner they returned to the Capitol for their candle-lit tour. This map includes pictures of the main destinations on the Churchill tour - the Christopher Wren Building at the College of William and Mary, Bruton Parish Church, the Governor's Palace, the George Wythe House, the Williamsburg Inn, the Raleigh Tavern, and the Capitol.

Below are the sites visited by the party listed in chronological order:

1. *Governor's Palace*
2. *George Wythe House*
3. *Bruton Parish Church*
4. *Christopher Wren Building*
5. *Raleigh Tavern*
6. *Williamsburg Inn*
7. *Capitol*

Map courtesy of The Colonial Williamsburg Foundation

This photograph shows part of the Churchill party exiting the rear of the Governor's Palace. At front (L to R) are Kenneth Chorley, President of Colonial Williamsburg, Winston Churchill, General Dwight Eisenhower, and B.W. Norton, Vice President of Colonial Williamsburg. They are followed by Eisenhower's wife, Mamie (between Chorley and Churchill) and former Virginia Governor Colgate Darden (between Churchill and Eisenhower). Behind Governor Darden is Field Marshal Sir Henry Maitland Wilson, to his right (R to L), Mrs. William (Eva) Tuck, wife of the current Virginia Governor, Mrs. Kenneth (Jean) Chorley, and John D. Rockefeller, III. At the top of the stairs to the far left is Mrs. John D. (Blanchette) Rockefeller, III.

After touring the Governor's Palace in Colonial Williamsburg, the Churchill party is photographed heading to the Palace Gardens at the rear of the Palace. Front Row: (L to R) Kenneth Chorley, President of Colonial Williamsburg, Winston Churchill, John D. Rockefeller, III, and General Dwight Eisenhower; second row (L to R): Mr. James Guthrie (to Chorley's right), Clementine Churchill, wife of Winston Churchill (over Churchill's right shoulder), and Mamie Eisenhower, wife of General Eisenhower; in the background (and only partially visible), Mrs. John D. Rockefeller, III (between Mr. Guthrie and Kenneth Chorley), Mrs. Colgate Darden (over Clementine Churchill's right shoulder), Captain Craig Cannon, Eisenhower's aide (directly behind Mrs. Eisenhower), Field Marshal Sir Henry Maitland Wilson (over Mrs. Eisenhower's left shoulder), Former Virginia Governor Colgate Darden (over Rockefeller's right shoulder), and Major John Miller, Field Marshal Wilson's aide (over Mrs. Darden's right shoulder). The gentlemen on the steps, as well as the uniformed police officer at the far right and the gentleman behind him are unidentified.

Members of the Churchill party pause on the steps of the Governor's Palace gardens to pose for photographers. Standing on the front row are (L to R) Clementine Churchill, Winston Churchill, Mamie Eisenhower, and General Dwight Eisenhower. Second row (L to R) Kenneth Chorley, President of Colonial Williamsburg; Mrs. William Tuck, wife of the current Virginia Governor; Sarah Churchill Oliver, daughter of Winston Churchill, Captain C. Craig Cannon, aide to General Eisenhower, Field Marshall Sir Henry Maitland Wilson, John D. Rockefeller III, and former Virginia Governor Colgate Darden. The guard at the far right is unidentified. Remarkably, even though everyone else is looking off in different directions, Winston Churchill strikes a classic pose, looking directly at the camera.

To begin their tour of Colonial Williamsburg, a restoration project financed by John D. Rockefeller, Jr., the members of the party motored from the train siding to the Governor's Palace, home of the British Governor more that 330 years ago when Virginia was a British colony. Their route took them east on Lafayette Street, south on North England Street, east on Nicholson Street, south on Queen's Street, then west on Duke of Gloucester Street to the Palace Green. (See map on pp. 84-85.) Crowds of William and Mary college students and townspeople lined Duke of Gloucester Street, waving British and American flags, as the party members began their tour. They were greeted at the Governor's Palace by Mr. and Mrs. John D. Rockefeller, III. Forsythia was in full bloom, and the sun was shining. As the group posed for pictures on the steps of the Palace Gardens to the rear of the Palace, Mrs. Churchill, a lover of flowers, was captivated by the formal gardens, and at one point was seen to gesture and remark on the lovely daffodils.

A Change of Plans

When the group left the Governor's Palace at around 4:20 P.M., four horse-drawn 18th century carriages were lined up to carry the visitors first to the Capitol, then on to Bruton Parish Church. Mr. Churchill and General Eisenhower climbed into the first of the carriages, driven by Benjamin Spraggins, Sr. However, the milling crowds and photographers' flash bulbs apparently spooked one of the sleek gray horses, a recent addition to the stables and not used to large and active crowds. It reared and plunged into the crowd, bowling over several spectators, backing the carriage through a guard chain, and breaking the tongue of the hitch, before handlers could quiet the animal. Even Field Marshal Wilson tried to help by grabbing the horse's reins. Churchill, apparently unperturbed by the incident, sat puffing his cigar and giving his "victory" sign, while General Eisenhower seemed worried about Churchill's safety. Fortunately the only casualties of the episode were the horse, who suffered a cut on his leg, and plans for the carriage rides, which were summarily abandoned.

Churchill and Eisenhower descended from the carriage with shouting mobs of spectators swarming around them and causing the party to take refuge in the nearby George Wythe House. As they walked to the building, dozens of spectators, mainly small boys, forced their way through the police cordon to shake hands with General Eisenhower. Once the police had gained control of the crowd and cleared a path to the parish house,

---

OPPOSITE: On leaving the Governor's Palace, members of the Churchill party are scheduled to continue their tour of the restored areas of Colonial Williamsburg in horse-drawn carriages, which await them in front of the Palace. Winston Churchill and General Eisenhower board the first carriage, driven by Benjamin Spraggins, Sr. Brief moments after this picture was taken, the horses, frightened by the crowd and by the flash of photographers' bulbs, rear and bolt. Officials, taking no chances with their illustrious guests, decide against continuing the tour by carriage. So, this is a rare picture, as the carriage "ride" was such a fleeting event.

RIGHT: After a brief stop at the George Wythe House and a tour of Bruton Parish Church, the Churchill entourage makes its way by car to the end of Duke of Gloucester Street for a tour of the Christopher Wren Building at the College of William and Mary. Here Winston Churchill (left) and General Eisenhower (right), in the company of John D. Rockefeller, III (center), son of the man who funded the restoration of Colonial Williamsburg, are photographed as they arrive at the college. Churchill sports his classic cigar, while Frank Dementi captures an exceptional picture of Eisenhower's famous smile. Through the window of the vehicle, one can see the face of an unidentified sailor, one of the crowd waiting to welcome the dignitaries to the campus.

BELOW: In this photograph, General Eisenhower and Winston Churchill (cigar in hand) exit the car and are greeted by Dr. John E. Pomfret (hat in hand), President of the College of William and Mary. Standing to Dr. Pomfret's left are Kenneth Chorley, President of Colonial Williamsburg and to his left, a woman, believed to be Mrs. Pomfret. John D. Rockefeller, III stands to Churchill's right.

In this photograph, Winston Churchill (center front), accompanied by Dr. John E. Pomfret, President of the College of William and Mary, (to Churchill's left) strolls toward the Christopher Wren Building (the oldest academic building in the United States). The state policeman to Churchill's right is unidentified. Over Churchill's right shoulder is John D. Rockefeller, III. Over his left shoulder, Mamie Eisenhower's head can be seen as she turns back to talk with a woman believed to be Mrs. Pomfret. To Dr. Pomfret's left are some of the many William and Mary students who turned out to greet Churchill and Eisenhower.

the Churchill party proceeded on foot to Bruton Parish Church, where they were greeted by the rector, Reverend Francis H. Craighill. Music was being played softly as the party entered, and at one point, Mr. Churchill sat down beside the organist, commenting on the *"restfulness"* of the church. This occasioned Mrs. Churchill to ask him if he was too tired to go on, to which the reply was a *"no."*

Leaving Bruton Parish Church at around 4:55 P.M., members of the entourage motored down Duke of Gloucester Street to the College of William and Mary, founded in 1693 by King William of England. Here they were greeted by College President, Dr. John E. Pomfret, Mrs. Pomfret, and a crowd of students. As the Churchill party proceeded across campus toward the Wren Building, oldest academic building in the United States, they passed through an honor guard formed by the Blacknall-Chess Veterans of Foreign Wars. Understandably, General Eisenhower stopped several times along the pathway to greet and shake hands with the veterans. After a quick tour of the Wren Building, the party motored to the opposite end of Duke of Gloucester Street to see, by daylight, the Capitol which they would tour by candlelight late in the evening. Then they drove back to the Raleigh Tavern, where Kenneth Chorley, President of Colonial Williamsburg, and his wife, Jean, were hosting a "tea" for the visitors. The time was then around 5:20 P.M.

Frank Dementi's Big Opportunity

Gathered in front of the Raleigh Tavern as the Churchill party entered were some two hundred journalists and photographers. Among them was Richmond photographer Frank Dementi, there at the specific suggestion of Clementine Churchill. As the reporters milled around outside of the tavern, inside, in the Tap Room of the tavern, the men of the party were being served liquid refreshment in the form of Scotch and sodas, while the women in the party were refreshed with tea in the Apollo Room. A man came to the door of the tavern and requested, *"Would Frank Dementi please come in?"* Intimidated by the crowd and by the awesome assemblage of important persons within, Frank ignored the summons. It was delivered a second time in the person of Inspector Williams of Scotland Yard, Churchill's bodyguard. This time Frank responded, creating an understandable consternation and vociferous grumbling among the other newsmen.

Leaving the College of William and Mary, the Churchill party motors back up the Duke of Gloucester Street, first to the Capitol, then to the Raleigh Tavern for refreshments. This photograph of the Raleigh Tavern, with a posed model at left, taken by Frank Dementi on an earlier occasion, gives a clear unobstructed view of the building. On March 8, 1946, some 200 reporters and photographers were gathered outside the tavern waiting for their news stories about the dignitaries assembled inside. Only Frank Dementi, by special invitation, was allowed inside to obtain exclusive photos of the social gathering. In the five photos which follow (pp. 98-107), Frank captured in magnificent fashion, the mood and character of the participants in that historic gathering.

The women of the Churchill party are entertained in the Apollo Room of the Raleigh Tavern at a tea hosted by Mr. and Mrs. Kenneth Chorley. In this picture, Clementine Churchill, wife of Winston Churchill, is served by Gertrude Ball, an employee of Colonial Williamsburg. (Exclusive photograph by Frank Dementi)

At the tea in the Raleigh Tavern, hosted by Mr. and Mrs. Kenneth Chorley, Mamie Eisenhower (L), wife of General Dwight Eisenhower, and Constance Dupont Darden, wife of former Virginia Governor Colgate Darden, are seen in this picture being served tea in the Apollo Room by Gertrude Ball, an employee of Colonial Williamsburg. (Exclusive photograph by Frank Dementi)

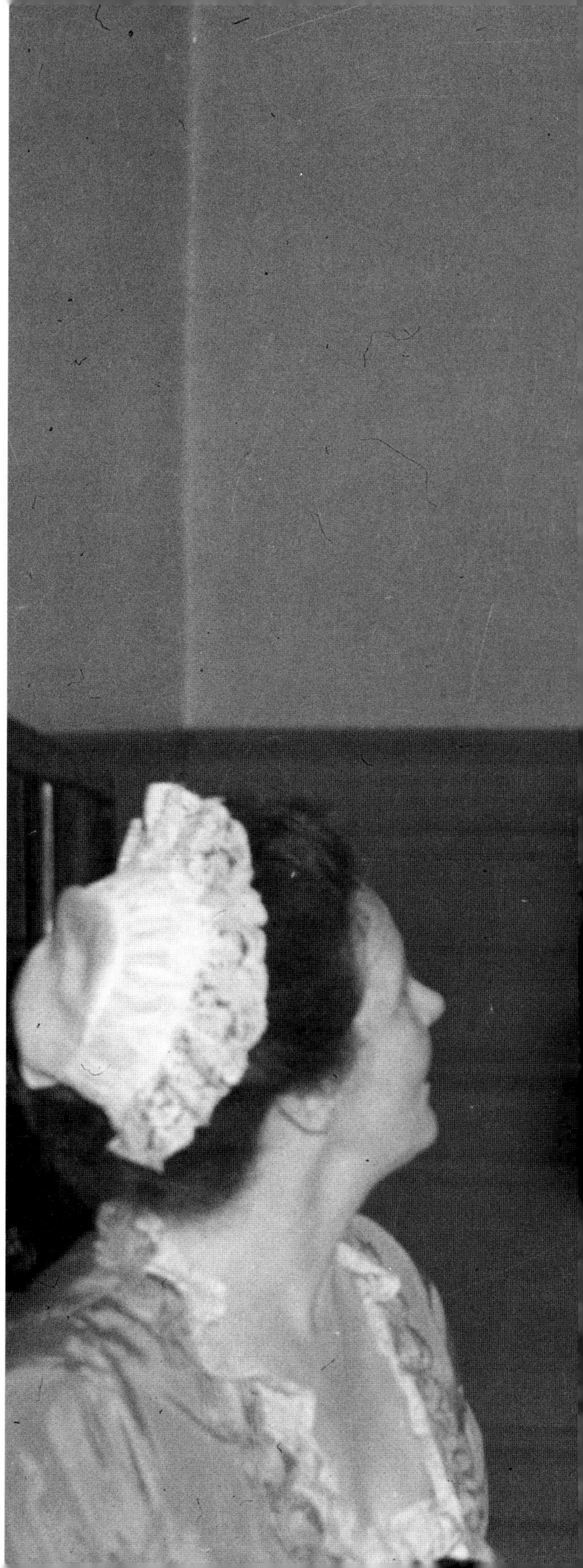

While the women of the Churchill entourage are served tea in the Apollo Room of the Raleigh Tavern, the men of the party assemble in the Tap Room of the tavern. Their beverage is Scotch and soda. In this photograph, Winston Churchill is served a drink by Willard (Casey) Casselle, head waiter at the Raleigh Tavern. To Churchill's right is John D. Rockefeller, III. (Exclusive photograph by Frank Dementi)

Winston Churchill and General Dwight Eisenhower relax in each other's company over Scotch and sodas in the Tap Room of the Raleigh Tavern, in an atmosphere far different from that of their numerous World War II interactions. Other members of the party are (L to R) John D. Rockefeller, III, Field Marshal Sir Henry Maitland Wilson (who succeeded Eisenhower during World War II as Allied Commander in the Mediterranean when Eisenhower became Supreme Allied Commander), and Former Virginia Governor Colgate Darden. The time on Eisenhower's watch reads 5:35 (P.M.). (Exclusive photo by Frank Dementi)

Note: A mounted print of this photo, autographed by Frank Dementi, hangs in our den. From this picture, some years ago, Robert N. Johnson, a friend and high school classmate who received an appointment to and graduated from West Point and went on to become a prominent Richmond attorney, was able to identify the ring on Eisenhower's left hand as his West Point ring.

- Brian Dementi

As the men in the Churchill party enjoy each others company in the Tap Room of the Raleigh Tavern, they pose with Williamsburg clay pipes for photographer Frank Dementi. A relaxed Winston Churchill is seated in the right foreground of the picture. Seated behind him are (L to R) General Dwight Eisenhower, former Virginia Governor Colgate Darden, and Field Marshal Sir Henry Maitland Wilson. Standing behind the table are (L to R) Captain C. Craig Cannon, General Eisenhower's aide; Vernon Geddy, 1st Vice-President of the Colonial Williamsburg Foundation; James L. Coger, Curator for Colonial Williamsburg; and Major John Miller, aide to Field Marshal Wilson. (Exclusive photo by Frank Dementi)

Inside, Frank was ushered into the room where Mr. Churchill, General Eisenhower, Field Marshal Wilson, Colgate Darden, John D. Rockefeller, officials of Colonial Williamsburg (Kenneth Chorley, Vernon Geddy, A. Edward Kendrew, Bela W. Norton, James L. Coger, Edward P. Alexander, T. Rutherford Goodwin, and James L. Coger) and Wilson's and Eisenhower's military aides were fraternizing. After some moments, Winston Churchill, sensing Dementi's apprehension, said, *"I think this man needs a drink,"* and called over waiter, Willard Casselle, who was carrying a tray of Scotch and sodas. At the invitation, Frank grabbed one in each hand and hastily downed them. Then the august assemblage of dignitaries welcomed Frank into their midst, and at ease now, he began to pictorially record this unique moment in history, when two of the greatest figures of World War II could actually relax and enjoy each other's company free from the strains and hardship of battle. The results were a photographer's dream come true. [12] (But this could hardly be said of the other photographers' reactions as he came back outside.)

Dream Dinner

At 6:10 P.M., the group left the Raleigh Tavern to drive to the Williamsburg Inn, where the Union Jack hung over its entrance, along with the Stars and Stripes and the Virginia flag. There everyone rested and changed clothing in preparation for an 8:30 P.M. dinner given in their honor by Mr. and Mrs. John D. Rockefeller, III. Guests at the dinner included the official party [Mr. and Mrs Churchill (under the watchful eye of Inspector Williams) and daughter Sarah; General and Mrs. Eisenhower; Field Marshal Sir Henry Maitland Wilson; Mrs. William Tuck, wife of the current Governor; ex-Governor and Mrs. Colgate Darden; Charles Campbell of the British Information Service; Major Miller, aide to Field Marshal Wilson; Captain C. Craig Cannon, aide to General Eisenhower; Harold Braham, British consul in Baltimore and Mrs. Braham; and James Guthrie, OBE, British consul in Norfolk, and Mrs. Guthrie (actually present?)] along with various Williamsburg dignitaries [Kenneth Chorley, President of Colonial Williamsburg and Mrs. Chorley; Vernon Geddy, First Vice-President of Colonial Williamsburg and Mrs. Geddy; Bela W. Norton, Vice-President of Colonial Williamsburg and Mrs. Norton; A. E. Kendrew, Vice-President of Colonial Williamsburg and Mrs. Kendrew; Mayor Channing Hall and Mrs. Hall; Dr. John E. Pomfret, President of the College of William and Mary and Mrs. Pomfret; Judge Frank Armistead of the Circuit Court and Mrs. Armistead; George P. Coleman, Williamsburg banker, and Mrs. Coleman; Mrs. W. A. R. Goodwin, wife of the late Dr.

[12] *Frank Dementi's various personal recollections of this event are collected and recounted on* *pp. 123-125.*

OPPOSITE: After an elaborate dinner at the Williamsburg Inn, hosted by Mr. and Mrs. John D. Rockefeller, III, the Churchill party leaves the Inn for a candlelight tour of the colonial Capitol building. In this photograph, Winston Churchill and General Eisenhower are departing through an honor guard of unidentified Virginia State Police troopers. Over Churchill's left shoulder is his ever-present bodyguard, Inspector George Williams of Scotland Yard. Behind and to Eisenhower's left is Charles Campbell, director of the British Information Services.
(Of note - this photograph was used as a clue in the Double Jeopardy segment of a Jeopardy program which aired on ABC on January 16, 2009).

Goodwin;[13] and Mrs. Marjorie Green,[14] whose husband John was in charge of the meal.] The dinner was an eight course affair which featured such traditional Southern cuisine as terrapin a la Maryland, fried chicken with cream gravy, Virginia ham, beaten biscuits, and fresh strawberry ice cream. The wine list included Cochran sherry, Louis Roederer champagne, extra dry 1928, three kinds of brandy, and three liquors including Van De Hum South African liquor. And of course, there were cigars and after dinner mints. [15]

Following the meal, host John D. Rockefeller, III offered toasts to the President of the United States, to His Majesty, the King, and to the Right Honorable Winston Churchill. After a few brief remarks from Mr. Churchill, in which he expressed his gratitude and delight at being able to experience "*the glories of the past, the pleasures of the present, and the hope of the future*" [16] all in the course of one day, the visitors were presented gifts to remind them of that day. The ladies each received a leather-bound copy of *Williamsburg Art of Cookery*, while the gentlemen each received a leather-bound copy of *Williamsburg in Virginia* autographed by John D. Rockefeller, III.

Dinner completed, the members of the party motored back to the Capitol Building, where they were given a candle-lit tour. Then at midnight, they boarded the special Chesapeake and Ohio train which had brought them from the nation's capital, for the return trip to Washington, D.C. (with a brief stopover in Richmond to pick up Captain Craig Canon's raincoat, which had been loaned to General Eisenhower during the rainy morning and apparently left in the motorcade car). A very eventful day was over. Two war-time friends had reunited and enjoyed each other's company, shared in the gratitude and adulation of an appreciative public, and cemented bonds between two countries that shared a similar heritage, vision, and destiny. For photographer Frank Dementi, his was a never-to-be-forgotten encounter with greatness. He would always have a permanent record of his experience and a tale to tell to his children and grandchildren (and to anyone else who would listen, for that matter). Because he printed up two of his exclusive portraits of Winston Churchill and sent them to New York for Churchill's (and Mrs. Churchill's) autographs (see picture, p. 125), his two sons would also have tangible reminders of March 8, 1946, a great day for Richmond, for Colonial Williamsburg, for Virginia, and for their father.

---

[13] *It was Dr. W. A. R . Goodwin, once rector of Bruton Parish Church and head of the Department of Biblical Literature and Religious Education at the College of William and Mary, who originally conceived the idea of restoring the historic area of Williamsburg and succeeded in convincing John D. Rockefeller, Jr. to fund the project.*

[14] *Mrs. Marjorie Green's recollections of the dinner, recorded in a captivating letter she wrote her parents the next day, can be found on pp. 126-129.*

[15] *The menu for the Rockefeller dinner at the Williamsburg Inn is detailed in Appendix V.*

[16] *Prime Minister Sir Winston Churchill of Great Britain. Archives of the John D. Rockefeller, Jr. Research Library, Williamsburg, Virginia, pp. 15-21.*

OPPOSITE: In the final phase of a very eventful day, the two old friends, General Dwight Eisenhower and former British Prime Minister Winston Churchill and their party tour the Colonial Williamsburg Capitol by candlelight before boarding their train at midnight to return to Washington, D.C. They pose in this photograph outside the Capitol, flanked by some Virginia State policemen and an unidentified employee of Colonial Williamsburg. Churchill's bodyguard, Inspector Williams stands behind General Eisenhower.

Sources of Information

Archives of the John D. Rockefeller, Jr. Research Library, Williamsburg, Virginia.
Final Itinerary For Churchill Party, March 7, 1946.
Prime Minister Sir Winston Churchill of Great Britain, pp. 15-21
Governor William M. Tuck Executive Papers (Legislature) 1946. Box 120, Accession # 24026, The Library of Virginia.
February 2, 1946 letter to Winston Churchill from Governor William Tuck
February 13, 1946 letter to Governor William Tuck from Winston Churchill
February 19, 1946 letter to Captain C. Craig Cannon from Governor William Tuck
February 19, 1946 letter to Lord Halifax from Governor William Tuck
February 19, 1946 letter to Winston Churchill from Governor William Tuck
February 26, 1946 letter to Governor William Tuck from Winston Churchill
February 27, 1946 letter to Jesse Dillon (secretary to the Governor of Virginia) from P. Solly-Flood at the British Embassy
February 28, 1946 letter to Jesse Dillon from P. Solly-Flood
March 1, 1946 letter to Jesse Dillon from P. Solly-Flood
March 6, 1946 telegram to Governor's Office from Field Marshal Maitland Wilson
Holleman, Joseph H., Jr. *Manual of the Senate and House of Delegates, Virginia, 1946.*
House Document No. 25. *Journal of the Joint Assembly of the General Assembly of the Commonwealth of Virginia.* March 9, 1946.
Richmond News Leader
Va. Senate Favors Bid for Churchill. January 15, 1946, p. 1.
20,000 Seek to Hear Churchill. February 19, 1946, p. 11.
Churchill And Party Will Parade To Capitol. February 27, 1946, p. 1.
Cadet Corps, Lee Unit Churchill Honor Guard. March 5, 1946, pp. 1, 2.
City to Clean Up Along Parade Route. March 5, 1946, p 1.
Parade Route To Be Clean, With Little Help of Public. March 5, 1946. Blue Streak Edition, p. 1.
Churchill to Speak on History Here. March 7, 1946, p. 2.
City Prepares To Welcome Noted Guest. March 7, 1946, pp. 1, 2.
Churchill and Party Tour Williamsburg. Flags Wave As Visitors Quit Train. March 8, 1946. Blue Streak edition, p. 1.
Mystery Donor Asks Churchill To Return Champagne Bucket. Blue Streak Edition, March 8, 1946, p. 1.
Churchill Waits on Private Car For Official Party and Parade. March 8, 1946, p. 1.
Ovation Given Visitor In Sweltering House; Eisenhower Also Speaks. March 8, 1946, pp. 1, 15.
Route Lined Whole Way To Capitol. March 8, 1946, p. 1.
Justices Face Hard Decision On Which Churchill to Face. March 8, 1946, p. 15.
Official Party Rolls Into City During Dark. March 8, 1946, p. 15.
Pair Greeted By Applause At Station. March 8, 1946, p. 15.
Soaked Cadets Break Ranks At Capitol. March 8, 1946, p. 15.
Williamsburg Tour in Plans Of Busy Day. March 8, 1946, p. 15.
Churchill, Eisenhower Wives Stay in Background on Visit. March 8, 1946, p. 22.
Churchill and Eisenhower Undaunted When Horses Rear with Their Carriage. March 9, 1946, p. 1.
Vandal Steals Page Signed By Churchill, Eisenhower. March 9, 1946. p. 1.
Churchill Sends Compliments To Richmond's Cadet Corps. March 9, 1946, p. 2.
Gen. 'Ike' Visits Jamestown With Churchill at Old Capital. March 9, 1946, p. 2.
Assembly Sidelights. March 11, 1946, p. 5.

Richmond Times Dispatch

Speaking Dates Held To One By Churchill. January 16, 1946, p. 10.
Vacationing Churchill Breezes Through City. January 16, 1946, p. 3.
Churchill Accepts Invitation to Visit Richmond for Address to Assembly; Eisenhower Is Expected to Be In Party. February 17, 1946, p. 1.
Darden to Go to Williamsburg After Address. February 19, 1946, p. 2.
Plans Made to Receive Churchill. Febuary 20, 1946, p. 2.
Churchill Visit Committee Named. February 21, 1946, p. 2.
Student Plans for Clean City Advance at JM. February 23, 1946, p. 7.
Five City Schools Are Invited to Aid Jayem in Students' Face-Cleaning Plan. February 24, 1946, pp. 1, 4.
Assembly Committee Lists Tentative Churchill Itinerary. February 1, 1946, p. 2.
Sound System To Carry Churchill Talk. March 1, 1946, pp. 1 B, 2 B.
Limit Is Set for Churchill Audience. March 5, 1946, p. 6.
City to Clean Route of Parade Today. March 7, 1946, p.7.
Limited Number May Hear, But Not See Churchill From State Senate Chamber. March 7, 1946, p. 7.
A Great Day in Richmond's Annals. March 8, 1946, p. 9.
Churchill Will Speak Here Today. March 8, 1946, pp. 1, 9.
School Children May Be Permitted To View Parade. March 8, 1946, p. 9.
Churchill Chats With Photographer. March 9, 1946, p. 5.
Churchill, Eisenhower Cheered By Crowds at Parade Here. March 9, 1946, pp. 1, 5.
Churchill's Unity Plea Is Renewed In Talk Here; Lawmakers Also Hear Eisenhower. March 9, 1946, pp. 1, 7.
Daffodils and Formal Gardens Highlight Mrs. Churchill's Visit. March 9, 1946, p.5.
Eisenhower Pauses to Chat with Man From Old Outfit. March 9, 1946, p. 5.
Eisenhower's Proudest Fan Stood Unnoticed in the Rain. March 9, 1946, p. 4.
Horses Bolt, Churchill Goes on Foot. March 9, 1946, pp. 1,4.
Rain-Soaked Crowds Line Parade Route As State Greets Eisenhower, Churchill. March 9, 1946, p. 5.
Text of Mr. Churchill's Address to Assembly. March 9, 1946, p. 7.
Text of Remarks By Eisenhower. March 9, 1946, p. 7.
Churchill's 'Reception' at Williamsburg Is Likened to London During the Blitz. March 10, 1946, p. 3B.
FBI to Return Champagne Bucket. March 10, 1946, p. 3B.
Register Lacks Signatures of Churchill, Eisenhower. March 10, 1946, p. 1B.

Virginia Gazette

Freshest Advices. Vol. XVII, March 1 - 7, 1946, pp. 1, 4.
Churchill, Eisenhower Given Hearty Welcome In City. Vol. XVII, March 8 - March 15, 1946, p. 8.

Washington Post

Ex-Prime Minister, 'Ike' Desert Phaeton At Williamsburg. March 8, 1946, pp. 1, 3.

RECOLLECTIONS

PHIL JOHNSON
As I Remember It....

Phil Johnson

On March 8, 1946, Phil Johnson was a tenth grader in the John Marshall High School Cadet Corps Band, which served as part of the Honor Guard at the Virginia Capitol during the Churchill-Eisenhower visit. His memories, as recounted in an interview with Dr. Brian Dementi, are presented here.

The John Marshall Military Marching Band was a very notable contributor to Richmond's efforts to welcome and celebrate the March 8, 1946 Virginia visit of former British Prime Minister Winston Churchill and General Dwight Eisenhower, then Army Chief of Staff (Supreme Allied Commander in WWII). We had the great opportunity and pleasure to interview as recently as September 13, 2012, a member of that band, Mr. Phil Johnson, currently an alto saxophone player in a jazz band, who participated on that occasion. Phil has been most happy to share with me his remembrances of that day sixty-six years ago. The John Marshall Marching Band in its formal presentation consisted of the Flag Bearers in the lead, followed in turn by the Officers of the Cadet Corps, John Marshall Cadet Band (led by drummers), and some six Companies of Cadets. The J. M. Cadet Band was military style and followed rules of an Army Band.

As Phil recalled, the events of the day proceeded as follows: The John Marshall Cadet Corps was stationed at *"Attention"* at 6th and Grace Streets for about an hour waiting for the visitors to pass in motor vehicles. The Cadets were standing in the rain, and it was cold. The fact of the matter is that it rained during the entire event. Once the Churchill and Eisenhower party passed 6th Street, the John Marshall Marching Band fell in line on Grace Street behind the vehicles and became part of the official parade, marching and playing military scores on the way to the state Capitol. Everything played that day were marches and the National Anthem; further, John Marshall was the only band present. [It should be noted that Winston Churchill and Dwight Eisenhower, joined by Governor Bill Tuck, were in a convertible experiencing the same inclement weather as was the crowd (this is supported in part by one of Frank Dementi's photographs showing Churchill and Eisenhower riding in an open convertible, giving victory signs to the crowd lining the street - see p. 57). The Virginia Historical Society estimated that some 30,000 people came out for this visit.]

Mr. Johnson explained that, as the parade entered Capitol Square from Grace Street, the motorcade proceeded to the right around the lovely monument bearing the statue of George Washington on horseback, from which point the parade went on to the South Portico entrance to the Capitol building. Once the visitors had departed their vehicles, the John Marshall Cadet Corps moved closer to the Capitol steps, and was located right at the bottom of those steps leading up the South Portico. Members of the contingent of those Cadets who played the marches had a preferred observation post at the bottom of the steps. In spite of the rain, Virginia's visitors stood at the top of the stairs and waved to the crowd, giving the "V" sign made famous by Churchill. Every member of the visiting party was clearly evident to the band. A particularly notable observation made by Mr. Johnson was what he termed the remarkable *"countenance"* of Winston Churchill as he stood on the Capitol's South portico, before the crowd. [Further, we might add, one photograph (see p. 63) of the visitors outside the building showed Dwight Eisenhower at attention, giving a salute, while Governor Bill Tuck had his right hand over his heart, which has led us to believe the Star Spangle Banner was being played; and we might now add that were that the case, the John Marshall Marching Band might have participated in the playing of the anthem.]

After the visitors entered the Capitol building, the John Marshall Cadet Corps remained at *"Attention"*, despite the rain, throughout the entire ceremony conducted inside the General Assembly Building (Chamber of the House of Delegates); that is, until after Winston Churchill and Dwight Eisenhower gave their speeches. Phil noted the John Marshall military uniforms were woolen, which despite the soaking, served towards keeping the Cadets at least somewhat warm. As I understood, at some point during the session inside the Assembly, the John Marshall Cadets were graced with an offer of hot chocolate, whereupon the order was given to *"Parade Rest"*(an official form of *"Attention"*), a change to allow time to imbibe the delicious and warming beverage.

After the events inside, the Churchill and Eisenhower party made another appearance at the top of the steps of the South Portico, where Churchill gave his "V" sign. It was unclear to Phil just how the visitors exited the Capitol building after the services. But at some point, the command *"At Ease"* was given, whereupon the Cadets could rest, move around and socialize. Phil indicated that for this March 8 visit of Churchill and Eisenhower, the John Marshall Cadets were *"very proud they could do these things - never any grumbling."* Further, ever since this visit of the Churchill and Eisenhower party, the John Marshall Cadet Alumni Band has had a social gathering once a month at Byram's Restaurant in Richmond.

[Now we should note that both Winston Churchill and Dwight Eisenhower affirmed a "soldierly appearance" of the John Marshall Cadet Corps: *"One of the outstanding moments of my recent visit to Richmond was when Mr. Churchill turned to me and remarked how smart looking were the ROTC units which lined the street leading to the capitol. I had already been most favorably impressed with the soldierly appearance they maintained despite the unfavorable weather. Consequently, it was most pleasing to have Mr. Churchill comment so highly upon your unit."* (See letter of Dwight Eisenhower dated March 12, 1946, p. 122)]

So, Phil's observations with respect to the John Marshall Marching Band on this occasion of March 8, were echoed by the observations of Mr. Churchill and General Eisenhower. Further, it is most pleasing to realize that as Richmonders honored and praised the WW II heroes, they were in turn watching us, rendering much praise upon our city, its citizens and heroes. Their attention to us, while receiving praise themselves, constitutes further affirmation of the greatness of those visitors to our city.

[Hooray for the appearance, stamina and military music by which the John Marshall Marching Band graced our city when it was visited March 8, 1946, by Winston Churchill, Dwight Eisenhower and their party, after the remarkable victory over tyranny in WWII.]

Phil Johnson
John Marshall High School
annual photo

CHARLES NUNN
As I Remember It….

Charles Nunn

On March 8, 1946, Charles Nunn was a freshman, recently come to John Marshall High School in February from Bambridge Junior High School. He was a member of the John Marshall High School Cadet Corps, Company B, which formed part of the Honor Guard at the Virginia State Capitol during the Churchill-Eisenhower visit.

It was only a little more than a month after I came to John Marshall High School, which was located at 8th and Marshall Streets in Richmond, that I joined the John Marshall Corps of Cadets and became a Brother Rat in B Company. As a private new to the corps, I spent a lot of time shining shoes, shining brass, and learning military discipline. I wanted to do well in the corps but the strict regulations of the Cadet Corps were challenging to any lowly private.

All Cadets in the John Marshall Cadet Corps received an official announcement from the Commandant, that on Friday, March 8, 1946, the John Marshall Cadet Corps would provide an honor guard on both sides of the street leading into the Virginia State Capitol. The occasion was the arrival of Winston Churchill, Prime Minister of Great Britain, and General Dwight D. Eisenhower, Supreme Allied Commander of the Normandy invasion on June 6, 1944. Winston Churchill was to address a joint session of the Virginia General Assembly.

At an assigned time, we were to assemble at Gray's Armory that was located on the corner of 7th and Marshall Streets. As I passed the large stone cannonball adjacent to Gray's Armory, I saluted as we were taught to do. Inside the Armory, we received our rifles and got in formation by companies. We then exited Gray's Armory in formation led by the John Marshall Regimental Cadet Staff and the Cadet Band with the Cadet Companies A, B, C, D, E, and F all in step, marching east on Marshall Street and then south on 9th Street, across Broad Street to the entrance to Capitol Square. We were directed to line up on each side of the street in the State Capitol grounds. A light rain began to fall but it did not bother us because we were so proud to be a part of this exciting, historic event. A large crowd had already begun to gather. We stood at parade rest until we were called to attention, and then we heard the command to present arms. Looking straight ahead, suddenly before me I saw General Eisenhower saluting us from his seat in the open car in which he was riding along with Governor William Tuck and Winston Churchill sitting up on the back of the convertible. Police on motorcycles were on each side of the car with two police on motorcycles behind the car. Their car was followed by additional cars, which I was told, included Mrs. Churchill and Mrs. Eisenhower and other dignitaries. After the cars had passed, we were called to attention, and the John Marshall Corps of Cadets marched back to Gray's Armory, stacked our rifles, and was dismissed. It was an historic event not ever to be forgotten.

Among John Marshall's treasures is a letter from General Dwight Eisenhower, commending the school on the excellence of its corps (see p. 122). Eisenhower also reported a flattering comment from Winston Churchill during his visit to Richmond. Today, 68 years later, a framed picture of this historic event hangs in a prominent location just inside the front door of our home. We want everyone who enters our home to know that I remember March 8, 1946, and will never forget that special day.

Charles B. Nunn, Jr.

Charles Nunn
John Marshall High School
annual photo

Elisabeth Ekstrom Dementi
As I Remember It....

Betty Ekstrom Dementi

Elisabeth (Betty) Ekstrom came to Richmond in 1937, along with her mother, brother, and father, who was a commercial representative for the Swedish tobacco industry. They resided in Windsor Farms. She entered St. Catherine's, a private girls' school, at the age of seven and graduated from there in 1948. On March 8, 1946, she and her sophomore classmates were part of the thousands who lined Richmond's streets to see the motorcade bearing Winston Churchill and General Dwight Eisenhower to the Virginia State Capitol. Here, in her own words, is what she most remembers of the occasion.

In 1946 Richmond welcomed and honored two World War leaders - Winston Churchill and General Dwight Eisenhower - with a parade, speeches at the capitol, and receptions. Our class (see picture opposite) went en masse to see the motorcade. We stood on the corner of Monument and Boulevard in front of First Baptist Church. The motorcade came from Broad Street Station (now the Science Museum) to the Boulevard and so to Monument Avenue. The open cars passed to clapping and cheers. At the turning into Monument Avenue there was some sort of hitch, and the cavalcade came to a momentary complete stop right in front of us. One of my classmates from Richmond, Connie Tyson (later Mrs. George Bryson), stepped up to the open car, reached out her hand, and said, "Hello Mr. Churchill, I'm Connie Tyson." I was awed by her bravado and somewhat alarmed - and I don't know what he answered or even if he did. The motorcade moved on and we went back to school.

Sophomore class, St. Catherine's School, 1946, from high school annual

Betty Ekstrom is sixth from the left on the next to back row. Connie Tyson is far right on the last row.

Courtesy of St. Catherine's archives.

General Dwight Eisenhower
As I Remember It....

Dwight D. Eisenhower
Photo by Frank Dementi

The following is a copy of a letter sent from General Eisenhower to Colonel Earl Brown, Commander of the John Marshall Corps, about the performance of the cadets in the Honor Guard on March 8, 1946.

WAR DEPARTMENT
THE CHIEF OF STAFF
WASHINGTON

12 March 1946

Dear Colonel Brown:

One of the outstanding moments of my recent visit to Richmond was when Mr. Churchill turned to me and remarked how smart looking were the ROTC units which lined the street leading to the capitol. I had already been most favorably impressed with the soldierly appearance they maintained despite the unfavorable weather. Consequently, it was most pleasing to have Mr. Churchill comment so highly upon your unit.

Please express my deep appreciation to all of the young men of your unit who participated in the ceremony.

Sincerely,

Dwight D. Eisenhower

Colonel Earl Brown, ROTC
John Marshall High School
Richmond, Virginia

Colonel Earl Brown
John Marshall High School
annual photo

FRANK DEMENTI
As I Remember It....

Frank Dementi

This is how photographer Frank Dementi recounted his recollections of the photo shoot in the Raleigh Tavern in Colonial Williamsburg on March 8, 1946, as published in the Photographic Business and Product News magazine's April, 1971 issue.

"You remember that Mr. Churchill spoke to our legislature? Well, two or three months before he came here I got a call from the British Embassy in Washington. They said I had been recommended to them, but I never learned by whom. I was told to go to the Williamsburg Inn, to the Information Desk, and someone would contact me. I went down, and sure enough a man contacted me. We got into a big car and went up to one of the restored houses. We went in and the man said, *'Mrs. Churchill - here is your photographer.'* There was Mrs. Churchill and her daughter. I spent the whole day with them, followed them all around, had lunch with them..........

"This visit was very secret. The pictures were put into a really beautiful album and given to Mrs. Churchill by the Colonial Williamsburg Association. I have to tell you about those albums - they were the most beautiful things I had ever seen. A few weeks before, an album salesman had come through. Those albums were unbelievable, they were so lovely. So I bought a batch - at $30 a piece! My wife, Connie, said I was crazy, but I just couldn't resist them. And they were just the thing for presenting the Williamsburg pictures to Mrs. Churchill.

"Then a few months later, Mr. Churchill and General Eisenhower came here to publicly address our General Assembly. All the VIP's went into the Hall of Delegates to wait for the thing to begin. Mrs. Churchill saw me and called me over. She said she had loved my pictures and wanted to get in touch with me that day, but didn't know when or how. Now imagine this! - there were dozens of photographers there, from all over the world! - and while I don't like to say anything bad about the profession, some of them were real nasty. But some got worse later.

"The party, after the speeches, returned to Williamsburg - to the Raleigh Tavern. I hadn't planned on going to Williamsburg that day, but because Mrs. Churchill had asked me to follow them, I went. I was sitting in a car, outside the place, when Inspector Williams of Scotland Yard came over and said I was wanted inside. I don't know what happened to me, but I suddenly couldn't move - I was scared to death! The Inspector went inside and a few minutes later two Virginia State Troopers came out and escorted me in. And here is where I found out just how nasty photographers can be. I had to pass through them, to get in. I knew how they felt, of course, having been in that position myself, but they shouldn't have said some of those things; after all, they sent for me.

"I was ushered in and there were all these big shots - and I just stood there. There was Mr. Churchill and General Eisenhower, Field Marshal Sir Henry Maitland Wilson, John D. Rockefeller, III, and former Governor Darden. After awhile Mr. Churchill looked up and said: *'I think our photographer needs a drink!'* He clapped his hands and a man came over with some drinks. I drank three Scotches and soda straight - I didn't sip one of them. And then I began to relax and from then on, everything was fine. I made my pictures. I copyrighted them."

With regard to the same occasion, here are Frank's comments to Richmond Times Dispatch news reporter Judith Davis when he was interviewed immediately after the death of former President Dwight D. Eisenhower, March 28, 1969.

In the article entitled *Seeing Eisenhower, Churchill "Scary,"* which appeared in the Sunday edition on March 30, 1969, Frank Dementi recounted his encounter with Dwight Eisenhower and Winston Churchill in the Raleigh Tavern on March 8, 1946. This is how his story was told to reporter Judith Davis.

" I thought I was going to die I was so scared," said Frank Dementi, recalling when he took pictures of former President Dwight D. Eisenhower and Winston Churchill that day in Colonial Williamsburg. He explained that some months prior to March 8, he had received a call from Washington asking him to be in Williamsburg, and on arrival, he found that he was to photograph Mrs. Winston Churchill and her daughter as they toured the Colonial capital. So when Eisenhower and Churchill came to Richmond in 1946, Mrs. Churchill spotted Frank at the Capitol and called him over to thank him for the pictures from the earlier visit. "She certainly did remember me," said Dementi proudly.

When the party left Richmond, Frank and a friend decided to follow them to Williamsburg to get a few more pictures. In the late afternoon, the group went to the Raleigh Tavern, where Frank sat outside in his friend's car to rest. Shortly, he was invited inside by an inspector from Scotland Yard, but initially he refused to go. "I was scared. I said, I'm not going in there," said Dementi. But eventually several State Police came out and ushered him in. "I still don't know why I was told to come in there," said Dementi, recalling the anger of the hundred or more news reporters waiting outside. "They never said anything about making pictures," but once inside he was offered a Scotch and soda to settle his nerves. "There were all those people. All of a sudden they just made me feel like I was one of them." He began to take pictures, and remembers that Eisenhower and Churchill joked with him about what was going to happen to him when the photographers outside got to him. At the request of Colonial Williamsburg, Frank made up six special albums, which were flown by private plane to New York to be given to Churchill and other members of his party before they returned to England. Said Dementi of the event, "A person couldn't have had anything nicer to have happened to them. It was the biggest thrill of my life." Frank copyrighted the Raleigh Tavern photographs and did not allow them to be published as long as Churchill and Eisenhower were alive. "I felt like I shouldn't release them at the time. I thought it would be all right to let anybody use them now," he said, adding that he was "real sorry" to hear of General Eisenhower's death on Friday.

After Frank Dementi made his candid photos of the Churchill party inside the Raleigh Tavern, he asked Winston Churchill to pose for a portrait shot for his two boys, Brian and Wayne. On the back of the autographed pictures he got as a result, this is what he wrote to each of his sons:

"Wayne and Brian,
I was the only photographer allowed to take pictures of Mr. Churchill at a party given he and Gen. Eisenhower at Williamsburg in the Raleigh Tavern in 1946. After making the picture of all the celebrities present, I asked Mr. Churchill to pose for a picture for my two boys. This is one of the originals I made at that time. Mr. Churchill asked me to mail them by air mail to New York, as they were sailing for London on the Queen Mary in two days. The signatures on the pictures were signed by Mr. Churchill and his wife Clementine. Always remember this is something very nice to keep to remember two of the world's greatest men and your dad who made the picture.

Lovingly, Dad"

Autographed Churchill picture

Marjorie Green
As I Remember It....

Marjorie Green

Marjorie Green, whose husband, John, was in charge of the elegant dinner for Churchill and Eisenhower at the Williamsburg Inn on the evening of March 8, 1946, was invited at the last minute to attend the dinner. The next morning she wrote to her parents, Arthur and Ethel O'Malley, in Palm Beach, Florida, recounting her experience in glowing terms. Her letter provides a charming addendum to the Churchill-Eisenhower saga of March 8, 1946. The following is transcribed by Brian Dementi from the handwritten letter. Our gratitude goes to daughter Joan Green Apter for sharing this letter.

Dear Mother and Father Saturday 3/9/'46

I could hardly wait until today to write to you to tell you the news of yesterday. I guess on(e) of the most thrilling of my life and I shall never forget it. At nine o'clock in the morning the phone rang and it was Miss Davis, Mr Chorley's private secretary who said Mr. Chorley wanted to speak to me. So when he got on the phone he said "Marjorie, I want you to attend the dinner Mr John D. Rockefeller III is giving for Mr Churchill this evening at the Inn. Be there at eight o'clock - wear a short dress and no hats." Well I was certainly almost speechless when I was asked as I knew all the plans etc. that had been made as John had told me and I knew the only ones from here that might go were Carrie Cale and Vernon Geddy representing Colonial Williamsburg. There were twenty four people on the private train (it was the President's private train) and only ten additional guests were to be invited - Mr & Mrs John D. Rockefeller 3rd who came down from New York to give the dinner, Mr & Mrs Chorley, the Geddys, Ex Governor & Mrs Darden and myself. I was to go to be with General Eisenhower's aide. So of all the people they could have asked, I was picked. To start from the beginning they have been working here at top speed for weeks getting ready for the visit. The Palace green was a picture, as a matter of fact the whole town - grass and shrubbery beautifully trimmed not even a piece of paper on the ground - Palace green & Duke of Gloucester street all closed off to cars at noon yesterday and the town filled with state police and secret service. The private train pulled in behind the Palace around two o'clock but Mr Churchill didn't get off until half past three as he was resting. He went directly from the train to the Palace - and we got a wonderful look at him - then he and General Eisenhower walked from the Palace to Bruton Parish Church and such crowds were here - went right past our house. Joan got so close to him she could have touched him. I didn't follow them all around as I wanted to be all rested for last night. I was given a pass to get to the Inn as secret service allowed no one to enter except guests who were registered after one o'clock yesterday. So I was all dressed and set to leave here at quarter to eight - and wore my black beaded dress and nutria coat and fortunately had had my hair washed and set on Tuesday. John took two sections of the Inn dining room, closed one off and made it into a lounge–small sofas and comfortable chairs, beautiful flower arrangements etc., so that was where cocktails were to be served. So when we got there stood in a receiving line first the Rockefellers then the Chorleys, Geddys, myself to wait for the guests to come in. The Eisenhowers came down first, and my they are charming, she is lovely. Then Mrs Churchill and their daughter Mrs Oliver, then he came in with Field Marshall Sir Henry Maitland Wilson and their aides. Well I tell you, I felt like I was in a movie. So after we had all been introduced we sat down and cocktails were served. I sat with Mrs Churchill for awhile and Mrs Darden and Mrs Eisenhower. Mr Churchill sat about two feet away talking to some of the men. He had a martini cocktail. Tell Father. Trays were passed with old fashions, martinis, Manhattans, Scotch highballs - anything you wanted to drink. Also sat with General Eisenhower and his aide Captain Cannon for I guess nearly fifteen minutes before we went in to dinner. He is just wonderful just exactly like his pictures and what a smile - told me he loves to cook and Mrs. Eisenhower said when she was so sick after having pneumonia last winter he was a wonderful help. Says he can bake a grand apple pie. At quarter to nine the private dining room doors were opened and what a picture - the table was gorgeous, flowers, Lennox China, etc. There was one waiter to every three people and first we had crab lump cocktail, then a soup plate of Terrapin Maryland, then breast of chicken with a sauce, fresh asparagus with hollandaise sauce, sweet potatoes, and all the relishes imaginable, brandied peaches, cheese straws, olives, celery, nuts etc. After that platters of Virginia ham were passed with mixed green avocado salad and cheeses, then finally strawberry ice cream and angel food cake and coffee and any kind of liqueur you wanted - brandy, Creme de menthe - anything - and the champagne flowed - the minute you took a sip out of your glass it was filled right up. Imported Champagne - Louis Roederer extra dry - 1928 - John says he has no idea of the cost of the dinner yet, but it is unbelievable. They even found out the brand of champagne Mr Churchill liked, his brand of cigars, etc. They got brandy 1867, sent the station wagon to New York to bring down the special liquors. The Terrapin was made in Baltimore - cost $150 for that alone, and that was only one course.

It took us about two and a half hours for dinner. Then Mr Churchill went to his room for about ten minutes and we all waited in the lobby for him to come down. Then we all got in special cars - secret service and police all over and we drove to the Capital. It was all in candlelight and we went through it. Then got in the cars and drove to the station where the special train pulled out at midnight. I saw President Truman's car - it was a five car train - a baggage car, diner and three private cars.

At the table I was seated one removed from Mrs Churchill and across from John Rockefeller III. Mrs Churchill is a lot like Mrs Rockefeller, so lovely and simple, you'd think you were talking to your next door neighbor and so interested in everything. She told me they were returning to England on the Queen Mary on the 24th of March. At dinner Captain Cannon was telling me all about Hitler's private train that they captured - said it was so luxurious it was unbelievable - all silver with indirect lighting, radio, telegraph communications etc. Said they had planned to bring it to this country for a bond selling drive, but the war ended so suddenly they didn't do it. My such charm - he was about thirty six and handsome, has been with Eisenhower for three and a half years, all through the European business as his aide, and my the way his uniform fit. Also, Eisenhower's - he wore a short jacket. Churchill wore a regular black striped business suit and had a cigar in his mouth most of the time.

When dinner was almost over, Mr Rockefeller got up and made a toast to him. Then Mr Churchill got up and talked for about five minutes and what a voice he has but he looked very tired - he is 72 years old, did you know that? I remember all the times I'd heard that voice over the radio and to be there almost near enough to reach out and touch him. I tell you I felt like I was in a movie - just think there were only thirty four people at the dinner. I told John it will take me a few days to come down to earth. John took Mr & Mrs Churchill to their rooms when they

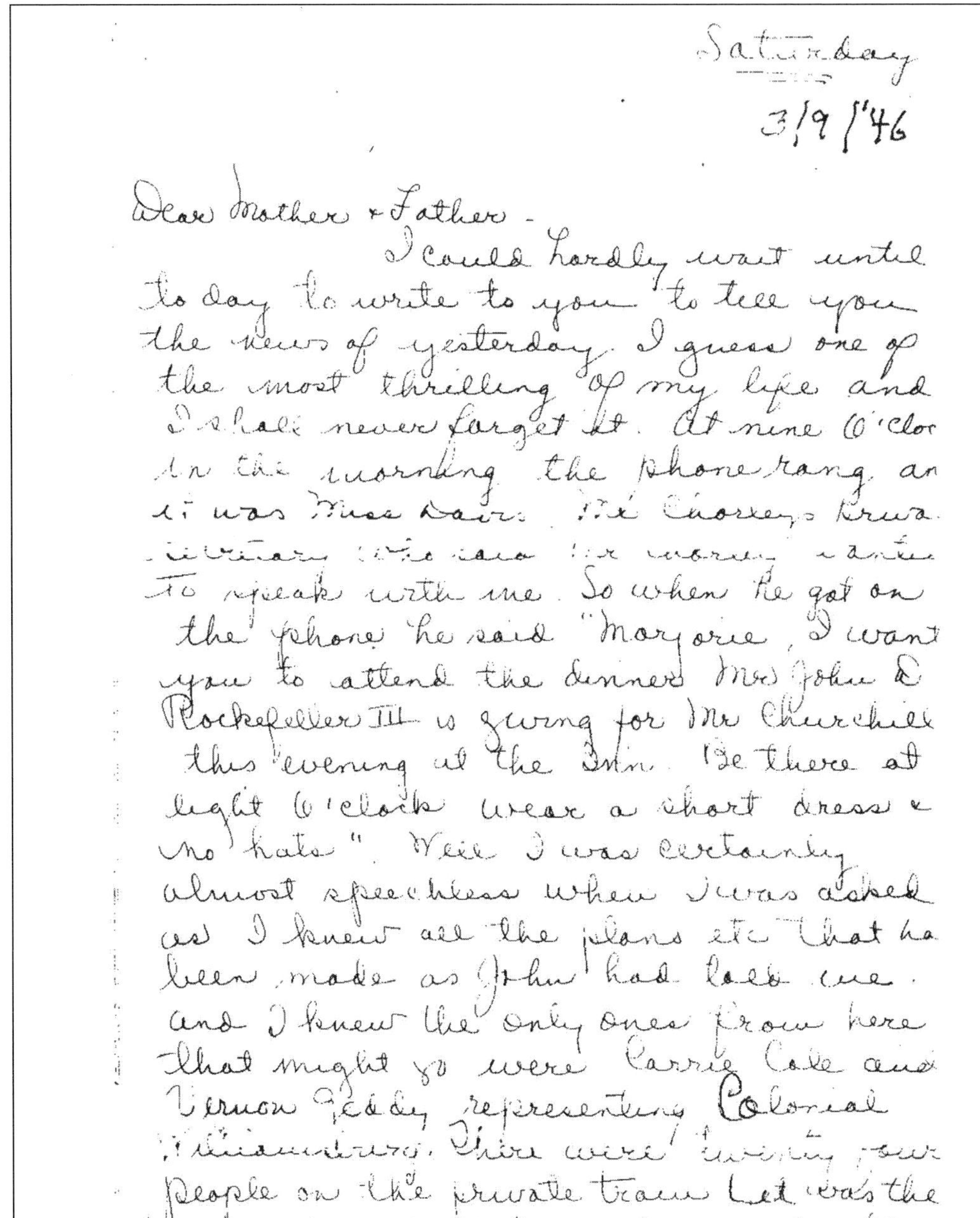

Saturday
3/9/'46

Dear Mother & Father -
I could hardly wait until to day to write to you to tell you the news of yesterday. I guess one of the most thrilling of my life and I shall never forget it. At nine O'clock in the morning the phone rang and it was Miss Davis [illegible] secretary [illegible] wanted to speak with me. So when he got on the phone he said "Marjorie, I want you to attend the dinner Mrs John D Rockefeller III is giving for Mr Churchill this evening at the Inn. Be there at eight O'clock wear a short dress & no hats". Well I was certainly almost speechless when I was asked as I knew all the plans etc that had been made as John had told me. And I knew the only ones from here that might go were Carrie Cole and Vernon Geddy representing Colonial Williamsburg. There were twenty four people on the private train but was the

ABOVE RIGHT: *A reproduction of part of page one of Marjorie Green's letter to her parents, written on March 9, 1946, the day after she was a last-minute substitute at the elegant dinner given by Mr. and Mrs John D. Rockefeller, III, at the Williamsburg Inn in honor of Winston Churchill and General Dwight Eisenhower. Her husband, John Green, manager of the Inn, was in charge of the dinner.*

arrived and Blaird took the Eisenhowers to theirs. The only other woman alone there outside of me was Mrs Tuck, wife of the present Governor of Virginia. Well they were all so lovely I felt just as relaxed and at home with them as if I had had some people in to spend the evening.

Well if I keep on this will be a book - could write you pages more about it - will send you some clippings

Lots of love to you all, Marjorie

The Chorleys left at 3 A.M. this morning for Palm Beach - should think they would be dead - think they will only be down for a week. Am sure they will drop in to see you. Tell Mr Chorley I just haven't come down to earth yet after last night. I'll never forget it but don't mention I told you price of terrapin or any of the details like sending up the station wagon for the liquor, etc. Also don't mention about the coach episode. It was his idea having the coaches, four of them, take the party from the Palace up to the college. Well he, Mr Churchill, and Gen. Eisenhower got in the first coach, an open one, and horses got frightened with the newsmen taking pictures, and the horses stood up on their hind legs and almost turned the coach over. All the staff tried to persuade not to attempt to use coaches, but he would not listen. Guess he wished he had.

John Green (above), Marjorie's husband, was the manager of the Williamsburg Inn and in charge of the Rockefeller-hosted dinner given in honor of Winston Churchill and General Dwight Eisenhower on March 8, 1946. While Marjorie was dining with the dignitaries, John was in the kitchen helping to make mint juleps.

Ramona Caselle Buford
As I Remember It....

Ramona Casselle Buford

Ramona Buford's father, Willard (Casey) Casselle, came to Williamsburg from Philadelphia in the early 1930's to work in the Civilian Conservation Corps, established as part of the New Deal Depression Recovery program. His six children, Willard, Jr. Ramona, Jacklyn, Jeanne, Lacanas, and William were all born in Williamsburg, where Willard lived until his death. March 8, 1946, found Willard working as the head waiter at the Raleigh Tavern in Colonial Williamsburg. It fell his lot to serve Winston Churchill, General Dwight Eisenhower, and John D. Rockefeller, III, there in the Tavern Room, where photographer Frank Dementi captured his historic encounter with the two war heroes (see photograph, p. 102-103). This is what Ramona remembers of the occasion.

As a child growing up in Williamsburg, Virginia, I remember going to numerous parades of dignitaries. These parades would start at the Capitol building at the end of the Duke of Gloucester Street and continue to the far end, ending at the corner of the grounds of William & Mary College. Both tourists and residents came from all over to this street to view the motorcades, horse drawn carriages, drill teams, and marchers, and to see bands perform. Often all of the local schools would participate in the events. Staff members would supervise and escort students to the parade site.

Ramona, Jacklyn, and Willard, Jr. Casselle, Yorktown, circa 1946

The dignitaries stayed primarily at the Colonial Williamsburg Inn or the Williamsburg Lodge. They dined at these same locations and at Chowning's Tavern and the Raleigh Tavern. My father, Willard Casselle, was head waiter at the Raleigh Tavern. He had the pleasure of serving Winston Churchill, General Dwight Eisenhower, and John D. Rockefeller III, during Churchill's famous visit to Williamsburg in 1946. I was 10 years old at the time and as usual, I was very excited to attend the parade. We lived only two blocks away from Duke of Gloucester Street at 322 Franklin Street, so as soon as we heard the sounds of any parade, we would gleefully run to see it. This particular parade was more memorable than usual because I overheard my father telling my mother about his experience in serving Churchill, Eisenhower, and Rockefeller. I was thrilled to see Churchill in a royal horse-drawn carriage waving to the crowd.

Willard Casselle, Jr.

Many years later (2008), my brother, Willard, Jr. was visiting an exhibit of Frank Dementi's photographs of the 1946 visit of Churchill and Eisenhower at the Williamsburg Regional Library, when he recognized our father in one of the pictures taken with Churchill and Rockefeller at the Raleigh Tavern. Excitedly he called the rest of the family to let them know of his discovery, since we were not aware of the existence of such a picture. Needless to say, we moved quickly to have copies made, one of which is proudly hung in my living room.

Joan Green Apter
As I Remember It....

Joan Green Apter

Joan Green was twelve years old on March 8, 1946, when Churchill and Eisenhower visited Colonial Williamsburg. Her father, John Green, as the manager of the Williamsburg Inn, was in charge of the Rockefeller dinner given that evening. Her mother, Marjorie, was a guest at the dinner. Their story is told on pages 126-129. Here are her recollections of that historic day.

It was just happenstance that my dad was even at the Williamsburg Inn in March, 1946. When the Inn was about to open in 1937, the woman who was going to manage the facility had a nervous breakdown. My dad, then thirty-seven years old and a manager of the Chatham Hotel in New York, was contacted by John D. Rockefeller, Jr. and asked to come to Williamsburg in the early summer just to get the inn going. Our family followed him to Williamsburg in September, living briefly in the Restoration House on Duke of Gloucester Street until it was torn down. We moved into the Repeton House for one year, then into the Dean House on the Palace Green. We lived there from 1940 until 1957, because my father's "temporary" job at the Inn became a permanent one.

Joan Green and family

I remember vividly the 1946 General Eisenhower and Winston Churchill visit. It was very special. They let us out of school early that afternoon (I believe it was a Friday afternoon). We went down to Bruton Parish Church because they were coming down to be taken through the church, and the only way for us kids to get a glimpse was to sit on the church wall (the part that faced the Palace Green). I remember shaking hands with both Winston Churchill and General Eisenhower, and of course that was just a thrill. These were famous people.

They spoke to us and they were very cordial. I remember President Eisenhower had a very firm handshake, and Winston Churchill had a very weak handshake, which kind of surprised me.

I also remember that my mother was invited by Mr. Chorley to attend the dinner that they gave for General Eisenhower and Winston Churchill at the Williamsburg Inn. Now Dad was "working it." He was in the background actually helping to make mint juleps. Dad was a wonderful drink maker, and they wanted to serve them something as a drink that would be typical of the South and of Virginia. So while Dad was back in the kitchen helping to make the drinks for the dinner, my mother was enjoying the dinner. Of course, she was thrilled. Here she was in her late thirties, and she was getting to meet these very important men. I know she was invited at the last minute. I think somebody couldn't attend and there was an empty slot, and Mr. Chorley was very nice and invited my mother to attend the dinner. So that was a special visit, indeed.

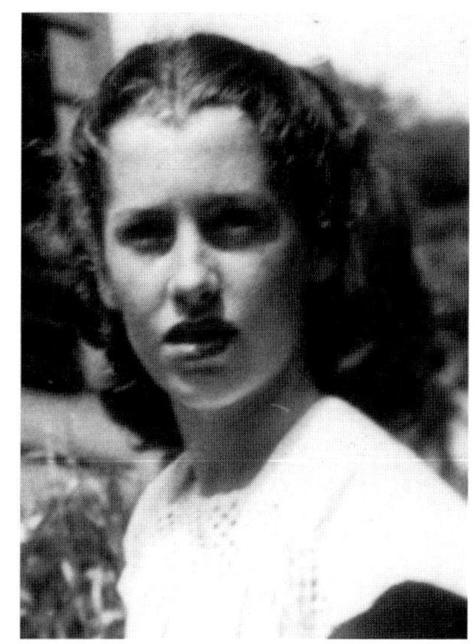

Joan Green, 1946

Brian Dementi
As I Remember It....

Paper delivery boy Brian and his dog Ike

Brian Dementi was a child of eight when his father, Frank, made his historic photographs of Winston Churchill and Dwight Eisenhower, so his memories of that day are from the stories his father told. However, as the years passed, Brian became his father's assistant and sometimes model on his photographic assignments. Here is his loving testimony to his father's personality and career achievements.

The following are some recollections of my experiences from a lifetime of being with and witnessing my dad, Frank Dementi, at his practice as an outstanding professional photographer, and in enjoying his humorous story telling. I might set the stage for this story as I remember him at his desk in the front office of his Colonial Studio located at 9 East Grace Street, Richmond, Virginia. It was at this front desk that Frank greeted customers and often entertained people with his photographs and stories of his photographic experiences. It was here that I remember his being visited by so many of his friends and admirers. The front office was adorned with all sorts of photographs, and other items of interest also hung on the walls. A notable photograph of St. John's Church, located in Richmond's Church Hill, resided as a photomural occupying the full area of the west wall of the front office. This photomural was a product of the studio itself, where the studio's staff printed Frank's original negative on large photographic paper and mounted it on the front office wall. Studio artist, Kay Nochta, then tinted the picture. This photograph was taken on a sunny, blue-sky, day in early summer, intending to portray a Sunday service with several parishioners (men, women and children) posed in colonial attire. The photograph captures a lovely boxwood-lined

St. John's Church photomural

walkway from the front of the church. Frank's desk was positioned in front of the west wall, so, as people talked with Frank, the picture behind him was very beautiful and relaxing. The photomural was so large, that studio visitors viewing the picture experienced a feeling of standing in the church yard among the parishioners. I should not neglect to say that it was in this very church, now a national historic landmark, that Patrick Henry delivered his stirring *Liberty or Death* speech March 23, 1775, during the inception of the American Revolutionary War. This photograph thus has the added value of bringing to mind Virginia's historic role in the American Revolution. The picture serves as an example of the literal host of such photographs taken by Frank across the state of Virginia.

When Frank sat at his desk the St. John's Church photograph was the backdrop. But other photographs and memorabilia adorned the walls. These included one of Frank's 1943 photographs of Clementine Churchill and daughter Mary Churchill taken during WWII in Colonial Williamsburg, and his 1946 portrait of Winston Churchill, autographed by Clementine S. Churchill and Winston S. Churchill (see p. 125), and accompanied by a note from Clementine's secretary, which read: "*Dear Mr. Dementi, I am desired by Mrs. Churchill to thank you for your letter of March 15 and to return to you herewith the two photographs which Mr. and Mrs. Churchill have been very pleased to sign for you. Sincerely Yours, (signed) Jo Sturdee, Private Secretary.*" When Frank passed these photos on to his two sons, he accompanied it with an inscription, the text of which is found on p. 125.

Other valued photographs on the wall included one taken a bit later in 1946, of Richmond's famous historian, Douglas Southall Freeman, entertaining General Dwight Eisenhower and Admiral Chester Nimitz at Dr. Freeman's home shortly after the end of WWII. I should note that Dr. Freeman often invited Frank to his home to photograph visitors who came to hear Dr. Freeman's expert accounts of R. E. Lee's strategies in the Civil War. There was also a January 7, 1953 letter from President-elect Dwight Eisenhower thanking Frank for his color photographs of Monticello (home of Thomas Jefferson) and Mount Vernon (home of George Washington), submitted on behalf of "Virginia Democrats for Eisenhower." From across the years, photographs of many other famous personages at times graced the walls of the front office including 1) outstanding photographs, candid and portrait, of Virginia's governors [inclusive from Elbert Trinkle (1922-1926) to Charles Robb (1982-1986)]; 2) photographs of John D. Rockefeller, Jr., Gertrude Stein, Henry Ford, Mary Pickford, Fred McMurray, Bob Hope, Doris Day, Gene Autry, Hopalong Cassidy, Martha Scott,

Jack Dempsey, Charles Lindbergh (and his Spirit of St. Louis), Admiral Richard Byrd, Lady Nancy Astor, President Franklin D. Roosevelt, General John Pershing, Field Marshal Henri Philippe Petain, Eleanor Roosevelt, Margaret Bourke-White, Mrs. Woodrow Wilson, and so many, many more, who, we hope, will be subjects of other informed publications we plan of Frank's photography; 3) photographs of brides and weddings; 4) portraits of businessmen and business establishments (e.g. Philip Morris, American Tobacco Company, Reynolds Metals, Thalhimers, Miller and Rhoads, Medical College of Virginia, University of Virginia, A. H. Robins, Byrd Airport, R F & P Railroad, Deep Water Terminal and so many more); 5) color photographs of scenes all across Virginia, from Tidewater through the Blue Ridge Mountains, battlefield parks, roadside apple stands during apple picking time in the Shenandoah Valley, Norfolk and Richmond Azalea Gardens, Gloucester Daffodil farms, etc.

In fact, Frank was a pioneer in color photography, and by virtue of his artistry, coupled with color photography, his photographs of Virginia's shrines were widely used to promote tourism in Virginia. Hence, one might see on his studio walls, photographs of James River plantations [Shirley, Berkley (including a large gold key to Berkley given by owner, Mack Jamerson), Westover, Brandon, etc.]; artistic scenes and photographs of many historic events that occurred in the tri-cities area of Williamsburg, Jamestown and Yorktown, dating from the 1926 visit of President and Mrs Calvin Coolidge, on into the 1980's; and many photographs of other Virginia shrines, such as Monticello, Mt Vernon, Stratford Hall, and others. News stories, or what might be termed photojournalism, also constituted a good component of Frank's notable photographs. And one could list here untold examples of photographs of unique human interest that might have found display in the studio at any time.

Monticello photo presented to Dwight Eisenhower

I should mention that during the 1940's and 1950's, as I understand, Frank was the only professional photographer in Richmond, and maybe elsewhere in Virginia, who was experimenting with, or pursuing, scenic <u>color photography</u>, and he was obtaining beautiful photographs of outdoor vistas and of Virginia's shrines. Letters that may have hung in the studio's front office praising his photography as promoting Virginia, could have been one or more of those he received from such organizations as the Virginia Travel Council, the Commonwealth of Virginia, Department of Conservation and Development, and the Virginia State Chamber of Commerce. As illustrative, the following is from a submission of the latter organization dated November 24, 1950:

"Dear Frank:

The beautiful color prints of the shrines of Virginia being published by you and Mr. William M. Brown (engraver) should prove to be of great value to the state. It has been established that visual presentation in color has the greatest impact on the minds of individuals. I am confident that the faithful reproductions of the Virginia shrines so intimately connected with the makings of American history will be impressive wherever viewed. Also they should prove effective as illustrated lessons in Americanism. We congratulate you upon this project and extend our best wishes for a success.

Sincerely Yours,
(signed) Verbon E. Kemp,
Executive Director"

(I should add that through the years, I remember Verbon Kemp as a regular contact often spoken of by Frank).

Located at his desk and at other readily available places, Frank had original negatives, color transparencies, and prints of a wide variety of his numerous photographs, with great stories he remembered to go along with the photographs. He was always willing and eager to share these with visitors to the studio. One of his favorite stories was about being boosted up by a man so that he could take a picture and finding out later that the man was noted financier J. P. Morgan. I cannot overemphasize at this point that <u>Frank was a humorist</u>, and was able to disarm people at large, bringing about their laughter at his story telling. His front office was "Br'er Rabbit's laughing place." Many people from all walks of life came into the studio to get away from their cares by having Frank show photographs and tell stories he experienced when taking the pictures. A good example which comes to mind, was Governor Lindsay Almond, who would leave the Governor's office, walk to the studio, get relaxed in front of the beauty of St. John's Church, and listen to Frank's stories. There were many others I could mention who came in while I was working at the studio.

Looking back in time, my experiences with Frank were many. The most remote memories were those associated with Colonial Studio at its original establishment on the Duke of Gloucester Street in Colonial Williamsburg during WWII. There were lines of army and navy men at the Williamsburg studio having pictures taken to send home. Between Richmond and Williamsburg, I witnessed long military convoys of troops moving through the state. At our home in Richmond as we sat at home after dark, we often had air raid warnings. A blast from the fire station sirens meant all lights in the community must be out. I witnessed at Virginia Beach, naval vessels firing anti-aircraft guns at targets being towed by planes over the ocean I remember Frank taking photographs at Fort Monroe (Old Point Comfort) and Fort Story (ocean front above Virginia Beach). As I grew up, more and more I traveled with Frank, helping to carry his cameras and other photographic equipment as we photographed many things of interest in Virginia. Time seemed to pass very quickly before I found myself driving Frank around Virginia, in addition to carrying cameras and related photographic equipment. (As it may interest some, Frank's mobile cameras, from among many, included a large 8 x 10 camera with fancy interchangeable lenses, a 4 x 5 Graflex camera, Rolleiflex 2 1/4 x 2 1/4 roll film, a German Leica 35 mm roll film, multiple lenses, exposure meters, film packs, flash bulbs, strobe lights, and so on. These could be quite heavy.) I fondly remember, too, many of the studio staff with whom I worked closely - James Anderson, Ahram Baronian, Pelham Duncan, Everett Nieunhause, Kay Nochta, Frances (Pullen) and Donald Pleasants, Brandy Rice, Jack Turner, and Jack Tyree - among others.

As to what we photographed, I could go on forever. As I try to mention certain camera subjects, please bear in mind that I am attempting to compress a wealth of experiences into a small space. In mentioning subjects, I should note up front that Frank had no trouble obtaining permission to photograph anything. Usually people were eager to pose for pictures, or have their establishments photographed, as back then, a professional photographer was rare and provided a way of remembrance and access to the public. I was around enough to hear about his photographs, and was present when many of Frank's outstanding photographs were taken, so that I can relate it to others. In many instances as I traveled with him I had great opportunity to meet and "socialize" with many owners or CEO's of Virginia's tourist attractions. The following accounts come from my own first hand experiences. I was present with Frank photographing the James River Plantations mentioned previously, and many other shrines including

The Sabbath

Monticello, Mt.Vernon and Stratford Hall. I learned of their history, witnessed their beauty, and remember the huge oak and poplar trees, and the smell of English boxwoods. I was present when he took many photographs in Jamestown (where he sunburned the retinas of his eyes capturing a sunset photo of the statue of Captain John Smith), was present on the Hampton Roads maiden voyage of the 1607 settlers' replica ship, Susan Constant, and was there for pictures of Yorktown (memorial and Revolutionary War battlefields), and Williamsburg (a huge number of photographs, including a most notable award-winning photograph which Frank entitled The Sabbath). [When I helped Frank set up to take the Sabbath picture, I told him he was wasting his time, advice which he fortunately ignored.] This art-form photograph was a hit in many venues. Colonial Williamsburg's appreciation of the photograph was expressed in the January 21, 1955 letter from Thomas McCaskey, Director of Promotions.

"Dear Frank:

Just a note to tell you something of the reaction we are getting here to your wonderful color picture "The Sabbath - Williamsburg, Virginia." I know that it has won several national awards and that you are getting very flattering comments from all sources, but I wanted you to know what we think about it here on the home lot.

"The Sabbath - Williamsburg, Virginia" completely captures the charm and informality of historic Williamsburg. Its quality, depth, and color trueness have caused more comment than any single Williamsburg picture that I can remember. You are certainly to be congratulated for this excellent rendering of a colonial scene in Virginia's restored city. It was a great pleasure working with you on it, and we enjoy sharing the acclaim that it is receiving."

I decided to specifically mention this photograph because it was Mr. Churchill's and General Eisenhower's choice to be together in the restored Williamsburg on their March 8, 1946 visit to Virginia, and because John D. Rockefeller III (whose father is credited with funds for Williamsburg's restoration) was named among the party of visitors whom Frank photographed on this occasion in Williamsburg's historic Raleigh Tavern. *The Sabbath* was filmed on Palace Green, and the home in the picture would have been seen by Churchill and Eisenhower as they drove to the Governor's Palace. [The diversity of Frank's aptitude and accomplishments as a professional photographer and personality are apparent, for example, when one compares, side by side, two of his Williamsburg photographs: namely, *The Sabbath* and his "Mona Lisa" photograph of Churchill and Eisenhower, relaxed and happy together, drinking Scotch & sodas in the Raleigh Tavern just after the end of WWII. (See photo on pp. 104-105)].

Paul Green's *The Common Glory,* was a Williamsburg amphitheater play rendition of the American Revolution, including Thomas Jefferson (portrayed by Laurence Hugo) composing and signing the Declaration of Independence. I was particularly proud when Frank photographed me as a youngster, shaking hands with Thomas Jefferson, while he was photographing the actors and scenes, as official photographer.

Another of my fond memories was Frank's photographing of a depiction of the Civil War surrender (General R. E. Lee to General U. S. Grant, April 9, 1865) at Appomattox. I assisted Frank as he photographed the large painting (circa 1867) of the surrender scene as it resides on one wall in the McLean House at Appomattox Court House. On this particular occasion Frank and I found welcome at the McLean house, where much effort was extended to accommodate Frank's camera and accessories. Furniture was removed to provide space to set up strobe lights, needed to enhance the image, which was hung at the time in a dark area of the room. The light-enhanced photograph was excellent, and the viewer can more readily pick out details in this very outstanding and historic painting.

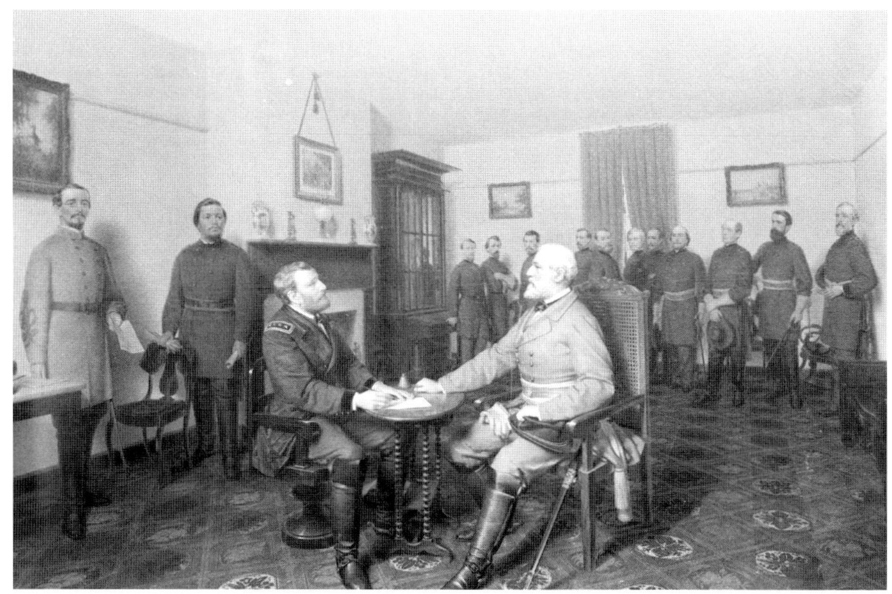

Painting of Lee's Surrender

I also had the good pleasure of being with and aiding Frank as he extensively photographed Natural Bridge, Luray Caverns, Skyline Drive, and the Blue Ridge Parkway. And in the latter places, I often stood with others as models in his photographs. These photographs were widely published and used to promote tourism in Virginia.

Other subjects for his camera lens, where I was often present during the photographing, included vistas in the Shennandoah Valley; Thalhimers and Miller & Rhoads store windows (photographs of latest fashions taken at midnight); tobacco worms among pile of tobacco leaves for American Tobacco Company; battlefield parks (Revolutionary and Civil War); and so much more.

Frank's Stories

Frank had many stories to tell, which I have repeatedly heard through the years, both at the studio and in numerous social settings. Since our publication is focused upon the March 8, 1946 visit of Winston Churchill and Dwight Eisenhower, and their party, to Virginia, I will give expression to stories centered around that visit. Accordingly, in September, 1943, in the midst of WWII, Frank received a call from the British Embassy, requesting his presence at the Williamsburg Inn on a certain day. While there was no indication as to why this request was being made, Frank knew it was important; and was present at the Inn as requested. As he indicated, when he arrived, there was someone at the Inn to receive him, who escorted him to the parlor. There he was introduced to Clementine Churchill, the wife of the then current British Prime Minister, Winston Churchill. Also present with Clementine was the couple's daughter, Mary Churchill. This visit of the two women to Williamsburg was described as secret and private. Frank was to be present during the visit for photographs as the women toured the British colonial capital. Frank has since described this as a wonderful day, where he had lunch with the two, got to know them, and was able to obtain many expert candid photographs of the women, who at times were joined by Williamsburg personnel. After the visit, Frank mailed to the Churchills in London a set of prints, decked out in what Frank described as very exquisite gold leaf frames. The particular frames in question he had had on hand for a good while, having obtained them from a traveling salesman. The frames had been retained in the studio just for an occasion such as this. As it turned out, the friendship he made with Clementine Churchill in 1943, opened doors for Frank down the road in 1946.

As explained in detail in this book, when it was announced in local Richmond newspapers in February, 1946, that Winston Churchill would speak March 8 before the Virginia General Assembly, and that he would be accompanied by General Dwight Eisenhower, Supreme Allied Commander in the European theater during WWII, there were some 20,000 requests for seats in the General Assembly, a chamber which would seat but 500 persons. When the event took place March 8 in the new House of Delegates Chamber in the Capitol, the chamber was packed with an estimated 600 persons, some in standing room only areas. I should note that, but three days earlier, on March 5, Winston Churchill, being introduced by President Harry Truman, had delivered his "Iron Curtain" speech at Westminister College in Fulton, Missouri. That event, which attracted national media coverage, likely increased public interest, and attendance, in Virginia on March 8, 1946. Frank was present at the General Assembly event, and in spite of the crowd, was able to move about with comparative ease, obtaining numerous photographs from a variety of positions, as the two guests entered the chamber and spoke. These photographs are among those shown in this book. At a point in time on that day, when Clementine Churchill was being escorted through the rotunda of the State Capitol building, toward the house chamber, Frank was able to obtain what turned out to be an excellent photograph (see p. 69) of the very lovely Clementine Churchill, with her escort. We believe it was at this point in time that Clementine, recalling the 1943 visit to Williamsburg, thanked Frank for those earlier photographs, while saying to Frank, "*My husband, General Eisenhower, and other members of the visiting party will attend a social event this afternoon in Colonial Williamsburg's Raleigh Tavern. You be sure and be there.*"

At 11 A.M. in the house chamber, Winston Churchill delivered his scheduled address. Immediately following his address, in response to calls for "speech" from the audience, General Eisenhower delivered an impromptu address. Both of the speeches are presented in Appendix IV of this publication. After mid-day, the party traveled by train to Williamsburg. Frank hastened to be in Williamsburg as well. In the late afternoon, Frank traveled with the party around Williamsburg, and obtained many candid photographs of the Williamsburg tour. These photographs are accompanied by good narratives. Around 5 P.M., the party entered the Raleigh Tavern for a pre-dinner social event. In Frank's account, as he was outside the Tavern among many spectators, including 100-200 photographers and reporters, the Sargeant at Arms came to the door of the tavern, and said "*Would Frank Dementi please come in.*" In his own humorous words, Frank said he was so nervous he would not go in. He has said he didn't know what came over him. A friend who was accompanying him said to Frank "*You need to go on in there.*" But before he could make any moves, Churchill's Scotland Yard bodyguard, Inspector Williams, emerged from the Tavern to escort Frank inside. The thinking was that Frank could not get through the crowd, no one realizing he was undergoing a neurological meltdown. Well, Mr. Williams escorted Frank into the tavern, as the other photographers/journalists raved. Once inside, Frank said he was so nervous he didn't know what to do. Everywhere he looked there was a famous face. Winston Churchill walked up to Frank, and perceiving his apprehension, said, *"I think this man needs a drink"*, and requested the server to offer Frank a Scotch & soda from a serving tray. Frank claims he took two such drinks, and consumed them rather quickly. This tended to allay his apprehensions somewhat. But then, according to Frank, the greatest thing happened. The visitors welcomed him into their fellowship, as if he was one of them, and very eagerly posed for his photographs. All of this, I might say, we believe was arranged by Clementine Churchill. We believe she liked Frank, and his humorous nature, and wanted her husband to make Frank's acquaintance. Frank then proceeded to make a set of outstanding candid photographs, featured in this book. (pp. 98-107) As mentioned above, at Frank's request, Winston Churchill posed for his portrait, two prints of which were autographed by Clementine and Winston, before the couple sailed back to England aboard the Queen Mary.

Winston Churchill and General Eisenhower were aware that Frank was the only photographer/journalist allowed into the party, and Frank indicated that both of them began to joke with him about what he planned to do when he got back outside among the crowd of other photographers and reporters. We believe there was not much, or any, sharing possible, as Frank needed to get back to the studio to develop and print his films. Further, Frank said at the time and later, that he was not disposed to let the photographs be published at the time of the visit. We believe he must have been very pleased with his photographs when the images came forward in the developing process.

Several days following the March 8, 1946 visit, Frank Dementi had a second opportunity to photograph General Dwight Eisenhower in Richmond. The occasion was the March 28 visit of General Eisenhower (Army Chief of Staff) and Admiral Chester Nimitz (Chief of Naval Operations) to the University of Richmond, on which occasion both military leaders received honorary degrees conferred in Cannon Memorial Chapel by the university's president, Dr. Frederic William Boatwright. Following the academic ceremony in the morning, the visitors attended a luncheon at the home of the university's rector, the famous historian, Douglas Southall Freeman. There were many dignitaries at the luncheon, and as in Williamsburg earlier in March, Frank obtained many candid photographs at both the degree-conferring ceremony and the luncheon at Dr. Freeman's home. Further, both General Eisenhower and Admiral Nimitz, at Frank's request, posed for individual portraits in Dr. Freeman's home. Frank received a very memorable personal letter (dated July 24, 1946) from Admiral Nimitz, on "Chief of Naval Operations" stationary, thanking him for a print of the portrait taken in the Freeman home. These photographs and Frank's stories that go along with the photographs are the subjects of another equally interesting publication we are planning.

In the early 1950's, at my request, Frank obtained a dog for our family. Because of so many photographic experiences and stories Frank had to tell his guests about photographing General Eisenhower, I named the new dog "Ike." I had a *Richmond Times Dispatch* paper route, and early every morning before school for about 3 years, Ike accompanied me delivering newspapers to some 125 homes. His greatest joy on those trips was sharing a quart of chocolate milk, which I often purchased from one of the milk delivery men (Curles Neck Dairy, Richmond Dairy, or Virginia Dairy) making their daily rounds. Ike also accompanied me each week during my house to house collection of fees for the paper. Ike became one of my best friends and companions. He was a very good dog. Frank made a photograph of me with Ike at my side (see p. 134), as I held up a *Times Dispatch* newspaper. The photo included my bicycle, with newspaper bag draped over the handlebars. This photograph itself is historic, in part because paper routes in Richmond are no longer routinely serviced by high school kids.

General Dwight Eisenhower and his wife Mamie came to Richmond yet again in 1952 when he was running for U. S. President. And once again, a notable collection of photographs of this campaign were captured by Frank, some of which may appear in a subsequent additional publication of Frank's photographs.

The USS *Dwight D. Eisenhower* (CVN-69)(*"Ike"*), a nuclear powered aircraft carrier (of the class Nimitz), constructed at the Newport News Shipbuilding Company in Virginia, was launched October 11, 1975, after christening by Mamie Eisenhower. At some uncertain time in the past, Frank told me, and I have heard him tell others, that he was approached, as I recall, by the United States Navy, to provide one or more photographs of General Eisenhower to go on board and be mounted on the new aircraft carrier. This request was probably received in the 1970's prior to the launching. I have every reason to believe Frank submitted certain of his outstanding photographs of General Eisenhower, and am pleased to express my pride that one or more of Frank's photographs most likely may be seen aboard the ship.

After the passing of former President Dwight Eisenhower on Friday, March 28, 1969, the very next day Frank was visited by a reporter, Judith Davis, with the *Richmond Times Dispatch*, to obtain an interview with him. Frank's fame at having photographed Winston Churchill and General Dwight Eisenhower back in 1946, was remembered by the editor, or publisher, of the paper, who was instrumental in pursuing an interview. Judith Davis' interview of Frank published in the *Times Dispatch* Sunday, March 30, 1969. The article, entitled *Photographer's Thrill, Seeing Eisenhower, Churchill 'Scary'*, was accompanied by a copyrighted print of Frank's heretofore unpublished photograph of Winston Churchill and General Dwight Eisenhower

Connie Sims Dementi

sharing Scotch and sodas in Williamsburg's Raleigh Tavern on March 8, 1946. The interview quotes many of Frank's thoughts and remembrances of his experiences during the 1946 visit, and, hence, is another good source of Frank's first-hand story telling. We are very proud that the *Richmond Times Dispatch* so readily remembered Frank's involvement as photographer during the Churchill and Eisenhower visit to Richmond and Williamsburg some 23 years before, and immediately sought his interview at the passing of former President Eisenhower.

A contributor of inestimable proportion to Frank Dementi's success and accomplishments as photographer and story teller, was Connie Sims Dementi, his wife, my mother. Connie ran the business, did all the book keeping, paid salaries, waited on customers in the front office (which she greatly enjoyed), and went on trips with Frank, keeping him straight. One noted Richmond attorney, judge, and long term friend of Frank, once commented: *"Frank wouldn't have a dime, had it not been for Connie."* This was so true. She was beautiful, and a great worker, running the studio. She loved Frank.

Dr. Brian Dementi

Frank Wayne Dementi
As I Remember It....

Frank Wayne Dementi was a toddler when his father made his historic photographs of Winston Churchill and Dwight Eisenhower. But Frank's stories about that day, March 8, 1946, lived on, to be told and retold as Wayne grew up. Like brother Brian, as he got older Wayne also traveled with his father on picture-taking trips and worked at the studio. Here is how he remembers "Pop."

We have always attributed much of Dad's success in photography to his engaging personality. Genuine smiles and expressions are so very important to presenting people in their best light. Dad had a gift for making people laugh and pose for the camera in ways that would make you think the camera was not even there. One way Dad inspired these genuine expressions was by telling stories. He should have been on radio as good as he was in telling stories. We grew up listening to Pop (he liked for me to call him "Pop") tell the same belly-laugh-prompting story to any and all passers-by. So, storytelling was another gift. I think these gifts were complementary. As he told stories, the person on the other side of the camera would become so engaged with the story that they would forget they were being photographed.... and, so – the big, genuine smile.

As we celebrate Pop's photographs of Churchill and Eisenhower and enjoy the expressions captured, we know that his special gifts for making people comfortable and happy in front of the camera were in play.

It is known that children will follow in the footsteps of their parents. I believe one reason that you are reading, and experiencing, this wonderful collection of photographs and stories is because his two sons, Brian and Wayne, are picking up where Pop left off...being compelled to tell great stories.

It is true for me that the account of the Churchill-Eisenhower experience topped the list of stories Pop would tell. From the moment he was summoned to join the gathering inside the Raleigh Tavern to the explanation of how he obtained the signatures of Clementine and Winston Churchill for my brother and me, I know and can repeat every delightful detail. Just as the words of favorite songs stick with us for life, Pop's stories are equally entrenched in my memory bank.

I am most grateful to my brother and his wife for putting our shared journey into script. By the way, that trait (copy writing) is not one we acquired from Pop. So, although we may both be able to tell these stories to our children and friends now, the life cycle to family folklore is limited. It is my hope that you are enjoying a slice of life that can be shared for generations to come.

Frank Wayne Dementi
Younger Brother, born October 31, 1944

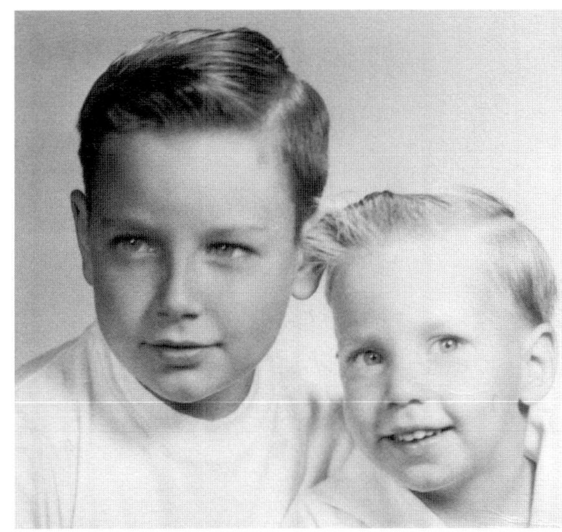

Brian and Wayne Dementi

Epilogue

The "vacation" of Winston Churchill and his wife Clementine during January - March, 1946, came on the heels of the end of WWII, and at a time when Winston Churchill, now a private citizen, was advocating measures to secure peace in the world in the face of what he felt were threats to such peace through actions of the Soviet Union. These views were enunciated in very strong terms in his March 5 "Iron Curtain" speech delivered at Westminster College in Fulton, Missouri, where the former British Prime Minister was introduced to the audience by President Harry Truman from a podium graced with the seal of The President of the United States. Churchill's address thus carried on the face of it, some of the weight of the United States President. Almost immediately, challenges to Churchill's Soviet views were published in a Pravda interview of Premier Joseph Stalin. Such challenges by Stalin were concurrent with subsequent speeches given by Churchill in Richmond March 8 and at the Pentagon March 9. There was some speculation that in response to Stalin's rebuttal, Churchill might modify his allegations in his remaining March, 1946 speeches in America. This dispute was raging at essentially the same time Frank Dementi had his rare opportunities to photograph former Prime Minister Winston Churchill and former Supreme Allied Commander Dwight Eisenhower, along with members of their party, in Richmond and Williamsburg, Virginia on March 8, 1946. Some review of what was being said by Churchill and Stalin is useful to the understanding of viewers now, seventy- plus years after the events, and it serves to accentuate the magnitude of the opportunity afforded Frank Dementi as a photographer in light of the historic moment. We have among Frank's photographs what is probably the first portrait of the newly recognized "Iron Curtain Churchill," and at Frank's specific request, it is autographed (see picture, p. 125).

So to come to a fuller understanding of the Winston Churchill of March 8, 1946, we should look to an analysis and comparison of his contemporary post-Fulton U.S. speeches as an indicator of his mind-set and his intentions. Towards this end, we include here summaries of Churchill's speeches, and a Pravda interview of Stalin, all of which occurred during March, 1946. The interjected commentary represents the author's viewpoint. The picture of Churchill that emerges is, not surprisingly, no different from that of the doggedly-determined war leader who would never let the British people give up.

"The Sinews of Peace" ("Iron Curtain") Speech[1]

Delivered by Winston Churchill at Westminster College, Fulton, Missouri, March 5, 1946

On March 5, 1946, Winston Churchill, wartime Prime Minister of Great Britain, addressed, by invitation, Westminster College in Fulton, Missouri. He was accompanied to Fulton by President Harry Truman, traveling from Washington, D.C. aboard the President's train. There were an estimated sixty journalists and photographers traveling along on the train with the former Prime Minister and current U.S. President. Many other newsmen joined them in Fulton. President Truman introduced Mr. Churchill to the Westminster audience, and the event was broadcast live over radio networks that covered the international community. The fact that President Truman was present and took part brought huge attention to the occasion. The address given by Mr. Churchill, *"The Sinews of Peace"* ("Iron Curtain" speech), as it turned out, created an international "storm," by virtue of his allegations of threats posed to the post-war world by the Soviet Union.

To begin the speech, Mr Churchill expresses how glad he is to come to the college to give the Green Foundation lecture, and to be the recipient of an honorary degree. He says, *"It is also an honor, ladies and gentlemen, perhaps almost unique, for a private visitor to be introduced to an academic audience by the President of the United States,"* thanking President Truman for taking the time needed to travel so far *"...to dignify and magnify our meeting here today..."* He assures his audience that the President has rendered to him the full liberty to give his *"true and faithful counsel in these anxious and baffling times."* The former Prime Minister says he has no *"official mission or status of any kind,"* and speaks only for himself - while yet citing his experiences of a lifetime in support of the efficacy of what he has to say. He says that the United States stands at this moment at the pinnacle of world power, which position is accompanied by responsibility for securing world peace. He advocates the U. S. and his country work together as English-speaking partners as they did during WWII. He would suggest that by working together now they could prevent another world conflagration, and should not let that opportunity lapse as was done in Europe by those in power between WWI and WWII. (I should insert here that in advocating such unity of English-speaking people to preserve world peace, he excludes from this notable effort those non-English-speaking persons who were critical partners among the Allied forces, e.g. the Soviet Union.) Mr. Churchill sets forth what he called an *"Overall Strategic Concept"* for preservation of world order and peace. This strategic concept has as its target the preservation of order against what he calls *"two gaunt marauders"*, namely War and Tyranny. He characterizes war as encompassing profound ruin. In WWII,

"The awful ruin of Europe, with all its vanished glories, and large parts of Asia, glares us in the eyes. When the designs of wicked men or the aggressive urge of mighty states dissolve, over large areas, the frame of civilized society, humble folk are confronted with difficulties with which they cannot cope." Our duty is to guard humanity from another war.

He then goes on to speak of a method ("*The Method*") to implement or secure the "*Strategic Concept,*" and this turns out to be a world organization - the United Nations - to enforce world order. This entity in his pronouncement would be equipped with an "*International Armed Force.*" He advocates that nuclear weaponry should not be a part of the arsenal of this world organization. Time is available at this juncture, he says, to develop a viable United Nations Organization before a new immediate threat to world order emerges - which it will.

Mr. Churchill then speaks to the second of the two gaunt marauders, namely Tyranny. He uses very stark language to describe the evil plagues suffered by ordinary citizens when police governments reign and overwhelm every principle of democracy - where "*The power of the State is exercised without restraint, either by dictators ....or privileged persons using political police.*" He says: "*But we must never cease to proclaim in fearless tones the great principles of freedom and of the rights of man....*" as set forth in several well known testaments of freedom both of U.S. and British origins, which he cites by name. Among these are the Magna Carta and the American Declaration of Independence (not saying that independence was from the British Commonwealth). He says such freedom and independence should be experienced by citizens of every nation - this should be the worldwide mark.

After commenting on what he calls the two gaunt marauders - War and Tyranny, he speaks of poverty and privation as widespread consequences of war, while yet asserting these could or should pass as nations work together towards "*...inauguration and enjoyment of an age of plenty.*" He cites another saying, "*There is enough for all. The earth is a generous mother; she will provide in plenty abundance food for all her children if they will but cultivate her soil in justice and in peace.*"

Mr. Churchill then approaches what he calls *"the crux of what I have traveled here to say."* (One might assert at this point that he apparently did have a mission in coming to America for his "vacation" or "health," a mission that was somewhat more than acknowledged, and that was to take the opportunity to speak to the world, to get off his chest, matters that bothered him, and to do it being introduced by the President of the United States. Maybe he hoped, thereby, to work to restore his image or popularity after being put out of office as Prime Minister following the German surrender to the Allies in 1945.) This matter of upmost importance was to advocate a *"....fraternal association of the English-speaking peoples. This means a special relationship between the British Commonwealth and Empire and the United States of America."* (emphasis added) This is followed by what appears to be a great wedding of the two nations which includes a complete union between our military establishments. There is a good paragraph or more in his speech characterizing the sort of intimate association between our two military establishments, and while he does not specifically refer to the term military alliance, that of which he speaks in my view qualifies as a military alliance.

Earlier he had supported a United Nations, and here, when advocating military association between our two countries, he dismisses any notion that such a special relationship between Britain and the United States would in any way infringe upon the viability of a United Nations Organization. He then says, *"We, the British also have our Twenty Years Treaty of Collaboration and Mutual Alliance with Soviet Russia. .....We aim at nothing but mutual collaboration with Russia."* And he says that this rclationship, and other special relationships between various nations likewise pose no threat to the unity of purpose of the United Nations.

He speaks of how all countries of the world must forge a Temple of Peace, and this must happen fast to prevent another war, rather than attempt to bring this about *".....a third time, in a school of war, incomparably more rigorous than that from which we have just been released. The dark ages may return, the Stone Age may now return on the gleaming wings of science, and what might now shower immeasurable material blessings upon mankind, may even bring about its total destruction."* As I see it, in this is couched Churchill' s fear of the use of nuclear science in war.

Churchill then says: *"A shadow has fallen upon the scene so lately lighted by the Allied victory."* Nobody knows what Soviet Russia and its Communist international organization intend to do in the immediate future, or what are the limits, if any, to their expansive and proselytizing tendencies. He says he has a strong admiration for the Soviet people and leaders, and can appreciate their concerns for military security from such nations as Germany (I would say at this point, the huge 1941 invasion of Soviet Russia by Germany, where the German army came within sight of Moscow, occurring in the face of a Soviet-German non-aggression treaty, argues for a Soviet defense posture of the grandest sort to guard against potential enemies. Churchill's ideas are idealistic given the proclivities of peoples and nations to be aggressive.) He advocates working together with the Russian people. *"Above all, we welcome constant, frequent and growing contacts between the Russian people and our own people on both sides of the Atlantic."*

What emerges next in Churchill's speech is that which I view as a second "crux" of what he traveled here to say. He feels compelled to make the following observation: *"From Stettin in the Baltic to Trieste in the Adriatic, an iron curtain has descended across the continent. Behind that line lie all the capitals of the ancient states of Central and Eastern Europe. Warsaw, Berlin, Vienna, Budapest, Belgrade, Bucharest and Sofia, all those famous cities and the populations around them, lie in what I must call the Soviet sphere and all are subject in one form or another, not only to Soviet influence but to a very high and increasing measure of control from Moscow."* This quotation, whether true or not, can only be viewed as very inflammatory with respect to Soviet Russia.

He speaks of what he perceives as increasing power and influence of Communism in Eastern Europe, seeking *"totalitarian"* control everywhere. He seems to be saying that at this moment while he speaks, Communists are seeking a communist or pro-communist government in the eastern zone of occupied Germany that would pose difficulties with the British and American Occupied Zones in Germany. He says: *"....this is certainly not the liberated Europe we fought to build up. Nor is it one which contains the essentials of permanent peace."* Because the seeds for potential war exist everywhere, still, we need the involvement of the (a) United Nations, now, (as I understand him). Mr. Churchill presents the frightful apparition that *"....in a great number of countries, far from Russian frontiers and throughout the world, Communist fifth columns are established and work in complete unity and absolute obedience to the directions they receive from the Communist center."* (Another very important statement with respect to Russia.)

He says he does not believe the Soviets desire war, but rather *"...indefinite expansion of their power and doctrines."* He speaks of *"our difficulties"* and *"dangers"* with regard to Soviet Russia which must be faced and not allowed to languish. He appears to be advocating here again the standing together of the western nations. Russians admire military strength, and do not respect what Churchill terms *"military weakness."*

Churchill holds in disdain the principle of *"balance of power."* So one must conclude he advocates military supremacy (or military strength second to none) on the part of Western democracies. He advocates peaceful action now to prevent another war, saying by analogy that such action during the 1930's might have prevented WWII. He does not seem to be entirely sure just exactly what the character and magnitude of the Soviet threat might be. At the end of his speech, he reiterates what has gone before as to the need for a "fraternal" wedding of British and United States might.

In summary, by means of this speech, Winston Churchill proclaims the United States in 1946 as standing at the pinnacle of world power, while advocating a fraternal association among English-speaking peoples, especially the British Commonwealth and the United States, to weigh against what he perceives as Soviet and Communist threats. He advocates a strong United Nations Organization, supported by Britain and the United States, to guard world peace. He identifies the "two gaunt marauders - War and Tyranny", and offers his characterization of both. He also speaks of poverty and privation resulting from war, and of how these can and will be overcome when peace on earth prevails - citing another who says the earth is a generous mother, when duly cultivated. He turns to the "crux" of that which he came to say - namely, advocacy of what he terms a "fraternal association" among the English-speaking people. This association in so far as Britain and the United States is concerned, is characterized by Mr. Churchill as essentially military in nature. He says that such special relationships among or between certain nations would only support the United Nations once in order - this all intended to preserve world peace.

While not saying as much, there appears to be a second "crux" in what he came to say - namely, that a shadow has fallen upon the scene now after WWII, which he claims to be the *"expansive and proselytizing tendencies"* of Soviet Russia and Communism. Then emerges his most famous statement rendered in this talk at Westminister College: *"From Stettin in the Baltic to Trieste in the Adriatic, an iron curtain has descended across the continent."* And behind this "iron curtain" resides a sphere of control over the nations in question emanating from Moscow. In his speech Communism is antithetical to every characteristic of democracy and human freedom. He says in part: *"....the Communist parties or fifth columns constitute a growing challenge and peril to Christian civilization"*. He does not believe Soviet Russia desires war. Yet he says: *"What they desire is the fruits of war and the indefinite expansion of their power and doctrines."* In the face of this, peace and avoidance of war is imperative.

Having read this speech, I see serious charges against Soviet Russia, which may lack clarity of Soviet intent and documentation. After careful reading of the text, I find no place where Churchill actually uses the words "military alliance" among the English-speaking peoples, yet his characterization of the "fraternal" association, or "cooperation" he envisions is crafted in military terms. In my view considering some twenty (20) passages in his speech, the wedding among English-speaking peoples is couched in military terms. Yet, he has abstained from use of the term military alliance. Also, the notion of a wedding of English-speaking nations, excludes Soviet Russia and other nations that were among the Allied forces in WWII.

"The English-Speaking Peoples" Speech[2]

Delivered by Winston Churchill at the Virginia General Assembly, Richmond, Virginia, March 8, 1946

This speech in Richmond, Virginia, delivered before the Virginia General Assembly, as recorded in the *Journal of the Joint Assembly of the General Assembly of the Commonwealth of Virginia,* has no title associated with its delivery; rather Mr. Churchill simply begins: *Mr. Speaker, Members of the Joint Assembly of Virginia, Ladies and Gentlemen* [note: the title *The English-speaking Peoples* was a title apparently assigned by James (1974).] Churchill expresses gratitude for being invited to speak, and gives some quite humorous comments concerning other speeches he had given before various parliaments. He mentions how on this visit to America he was invited to speak at other State Legislatures, including South Carolina, Kentucky and Mississippi. Yet he responded in the affirmative to the invitation from Virginia, saying, given the constraints of time, he *"felt that the other states would be willing to accept the primacy of the Virginia Assembly as the most ancient lawmaking body on the mainland of the Western Hemisphere."* He mentions his desire to visit Williamsburg on this occasion, and his hope that General Eisenhower, who is also present on this occasion, would *"pilot me around."* He expresses happiness to be with his friend Eisenhower on this trip here in the states, recalling his many *"connections"* with Eisenhower during the war in Europe. He praises Eisenhower and his attributes as he experienced them during the war. **Mr. Churchill says sort of humorously (perhaps on the heels of international responses generated by his "Iron Curtain" speech given three days before in Fulton, Missouri): Mr. Speaker,** *"Do you not think you are running some risk in inviting me to give my faithful counsel on* *this occasion? You have not asked to see beforehand what I am going to say. I might easily, for instance, blurt out a lot of things which people know in their hearts are true, but are a bit shy of saying in public. And this might cause a regular commotion and get you all into trouble."* (Comment: it would seem in this phraseology he is mocking those who may have spoken in derision of his speech in Fulton, yet he is not at all backing down from what he said on that previous occasion.) " *However, the people of Virginia and above all the people of Richmond, have proved in the past that they have strong nerves, and that they can face not only facts, but fate, with fortitude and pride."* He then goes on to say that in Richmond and Williamsburg reside that cradle through which over a hundred fifty year period, the great American republic was nursed.

Mr. Churchill speaks of the historic documents of freedom created here, while mentioning such notable Virginians as Thomas Jefferson, Patrick Henry, Richard Henry Lee, and George Washington. He says: *"The theme of individual liberty and of the rights of the citizen so painfully evolved across the centuries in England was upheld through every stress and confusion by Virginia, and that theme lights the English speaking world today."* (Amen!) **(Note it is here that he reiterates what one might call a wedding of English speaking peoples, perhaps as opposed to those provinces/nationalities where the freedom of man suffers recognition.)** He says: *"Mr. Speaker, I salute you here in this General Assembly as the guardians of the sacred flame"* (of the rights of man - comment added).

Mr. Churchill then advances forward some one hundred years in Virginia history, to that point where Virginia and Richmond resided at the center of what he termed the "tragedy." He sees this time attested to in many battlefields in the area, which he says he has visited in the past, guided by Mr. Freeman (Douglas Southall Freeman, full name added), whom he says is in the audience today. He mentions such Virginians in the conflict as "Stonewall" Jackson and Robert E. Lee. Seemingly referring to Virginians in that conflict, he says: *"Surely,....so long as men turn to the records of history will their deeds live, giving to all time one of the noblest examples of unyielding courage and devotion the world has known."* Further, he says: *"There was about General Robert E. Lee a character, a quality of selflessness which raises him to the very highest rank of men.....who are being concerned with the fortunes of nations."* Further, he spoke of Generals George Marshall and Dwight Eisenhower as having the same character, as well as others in the United States Army and Navy. *"Today the American Union is the most powerful champion of national and individual freedom, and it carries with it a large portion of the hopes of men."* During WWII: *"....she also acted as the great arsenal of democracy to the friends of freedom in every land." "Moreover, it fell to us* (meaning the British Commonwealth) *to have the honor of standing alone for a whole year against the main strength of the mighty Axis,"* thereby gaining the time necessary for the United States' military preparation. **Churchill advocates our two nations standing together.....***"in defense of those causes which we hold dear."*

Further, *"It is in the years of peace that wars are prevented......but peace will not be preserved without the virtues that make victory possible in war......Great Heart must have his sword and armor to guard the pilgrims on their way......Above all, among the English speaking peoples there must be the union of hearts based upon conviction and common ideals."* (Comment: In this passage, it would seem he is advocating English speaking people standing together, even in a military sense as I read it. Yet, he does not say against whom. Without naming anyone, the adversary would appear to be tyranny, and anyone who would deny men their God-given freedoms, even to the point of slavery. To the extent that the Iron Curtain speech identifies the Soviet Union as tyrannical, without saying as much, this Richmond speech would seem to support that speech of March 5, or indeed the two speeches might be viewed as one contiguous speech, petitioned or divided by a three day break in its delivery.)

Churchill levels great praise upon America in his time, as the nation beyond all others in which the world places great hope. This should always be America.

....

"The Anglo-American Alliance" Speech[3]

Delivered by Winston Churchill at the Pentagon, Washington, D.C. (Actually, northern Virginia), March 9, 1946

This speech actually took place in Virginia the day following Churchill's address to the Virginia General Assembly in Richmond and his visit that afternoon to Colonial Williamsburg, where he was accompanied by General Eisenhower and other members of the visiting party. Mr. Churchill indicates he was invited to speak on this occasion at the Pentagon by the Secretary of War and General Eisenhower (Army Chief of Staff). This speech incorporates much praise of the American military establishment during WWII. Certain basic aspects of the speech are rendered as follows: Mr. Churchill opens with an expression of his great pleasure and honor at being invited for this occasion. He speaks of the intimacy of the association between British and U.S. military personnel during the war engagement, where he says the English language served as a great bridge (so in this speech there are elements of the wedding of English-speaking peoples during and after the war). *"There are many, many ideas we have in common and also practice: but there was a spirit of loyalty, of good will, of comradeship which never has been seen in all the history of war between Allied Armies, Navies, Air Forces fighting together side by side. On General Eisenhower's staff, which I saw often and closely in Africa, in France and in Germany, it was carried to extreme perfection." "No one was more the champion and embodiment of this unity than General Eisenhower."* He says he has been told that the same sort of unity was witnessed among Allied forces in the Pacific. Mr. Churchill goes on: *"But it was one great force that overthrew the mighty powers with which we were confronted and which were dashed to ruin and helplessness by our exertions."*

He highly praises the rapidity with which the United States expanded as a military force upon entry into WWII. *" Nevertheless the rate at which the small American Army of only a few hundred thousand men, not long before the war, created the mighty force of millions of soldiers, is a wonder in military history." "I saw the creation of this mighty force - this mighty Army, victorious in every theater against the enemy in so short a time and from such a very small parent stock. This is an achievement which the soldiers of every other country will always study with admiration and with envy." Further, he says: "It remains to me a mystery as yet unexplained how the very small staffs which the United States kept during the years of peace were able not only to build up the Armies and Air Force units, but also to find the leaders and vast staffs capable of handling enormous masses and of moving them faster and farther than masses have ever been moved in war before."*

"That you should have been able to preserve the art not only of creating mighty armies at the stroke of a wand - but of leading and guiding those armies upon a scale incomparably greater than anything that was prepared for or even dreamed of, constitutes a gift made by the Officer Corps of the United States to their nation in time of trouble, which I earnestly hope will never be forgotten here, and it certainly never will be forgotten in the island from which I come. You will, I am sure, permit me to associate with this amazing feat, the name of General Marshall, the creator of this Instrument of Victory." (emphasis added)

In this speech, Mr. Churchill did not recall or embellish his warnings regarding Soviet aggression that he expressed in his March 5 Fulton "Iron Curtain" speech. This speech was rendered at the Pentagon (locus of the United States Defense Department), and was in essence largely a military speech focusing upon military accomplishments of the United States in WWII, while speaking as well of the coordinate efforts of the English-speaking peoples. So the speech seems to bespeak of, perhaps continuing, military alliance between the United States and Britain, although the phrase "military alliance" does not actually appear in the text.

We should not fail to note that Winston Churchill, and one person on whom he lavished praise as a military leader, General Dwight Eisenhower, had been photographed together on the evening before (March 8) by Frank Dementi at a social event in Williamsburg, as the two shared together fellowship and Scotch and sodas (see photo on pp. 104-105).

JOSEPH STALIN, PRAVDA INTERVIEW[4]

March 8 -10, 1946

"Stalin Interview With Pravda On Churchill" as published in The New York Times, March 14, 1946. The New York Times article begins: *"London, March 13 (U.P.) - The text of a Moscow broadcast on Generalissimo Stalin's statement follows:"*

The article presents this as an event conducted a few days ago, wherein a Pravda correspondent interviewed, or questioned, Stalin on the speech by Winston Churchill delivered March 5 at Fulton, Missouri (the Times article does not actually name the place nor provide the date of the Churchill speech in question, but the context of the article makes it plain - Stalin is addressing the speech given at Westminister College). It is to be noted we do not have the information to put an actual date on the Stalin interview. "A few days ago" would in a general sense be interpreted as 3-5 days ago. So the interview may have occurred somewhere between March 8 -10, 1946, which would have allowed for a timely Russian response to Churchill's March 5 Fulton address, and further, would have closely approximated Churchill's March 8 address in Richmond. So to the extent the Stalin response created a stir, by the 15th of March, Churchill would have had reasonable knowledge of Stalin's response, and reasonable opportunity to modify his views with respect to those espoused in Fulton. The first question to Stalin asks for his assessment of the last speech made by Churchill in the United States. This would suggest the Stalin interview occurred on or just after March 8. As to that point in time, the March 5 address in Fulton would have been Churchill's last speech with respect to this Stalin interview. Stalin's response to this first question: *"I assess it as a dangerous act to sow the seed of discord among the Allied governments and hamper their cooperation."* We would note that to the extent that Soviet Russia was among the Allied forces in WWII, his response is reasonable. The next question reads: *"Can one consider that the speech of Mr. Churchill is damaging to the cause of peace and security?"* In our view, this is a leading question. Stalin answers, *"Undoubtably, yes,"* while going on to characterize Churchill as a *"firebrand of war,"* and to say that he is not alone given his friends in both England and the United States. Stalin then likens Churchill to Hitler, in that the latter viewed that *"...only people speaking the German language represent a fully valuable nation."* Stalin characterized this as a German racial theory, implying that accordingly Hitler, or the German people, believed they must rule over other nations. Similarly, Stalin says: *"Mr. Churchill begins to set war loose also by a racial theory, maintaining that only nations speaking the English language are fully valuable nations, called upon to decide the destinies of the entire world,"* thereby maintaining that the English-speaking nations should rule over all others, world-wide. We feel Stalin's views expressed here are reasonable but deficient, as Churchill did place primacy upon English-speaking people as the world leaders, even though, and in face of the fact that, the Allied forces were multi-lingual.

Further, Stalin characterizes Churchill as mandating that <u>non</u>-English-speaking nations shall *"recognize our lordship voluntarily and all will be well."* While it follows that *"In the contrary case, war is inevitable"*, or we would say is perhaps more likely, we can see how this rhetoric would be upsetting to good peoples of other, non English-speaking nations. Stalin observes, *"But the nations have shed their blood during five years of cruel war for the sake of liberty and the independence of their countries, and not for the sake of exchanging the lordship of Hitler for the lordship of Churchill."*

So with these stern words as uttered by both Churchill and Stalin, the stage was set for a huge military-orientated confrontation shortly after WWII. Stalin feels the failure of Churchill resides with the fact that he does not understand the simple fact that non-English-speaking peoples, who make up the majority of the world's population, will not go along with some sort of subservience to the English-speaking nations. Stalin also sees Churchill as failing to recognize the veracity of the existing Anglo-Soviet treaty, advocating its extension while at the same moment characterizing non-English-speaking Soviets as somehow subservient to English-speaking peoples. He offers the opinion that Churchill's rhetoric is setting a stage for war against the Soviet Union. The notion of extending an Anglo-Soviet treaty while using anti-Soviet rhetoric in essence turns the treaty *"into an empty scrap of paper."*

Another question posed to Stalin, paraphrased as follows, in essence asks: *How do you assess Churchill's attacking democratic regimes of those countries which are good neighbors of the Soviet Union?* Stalin answers that Churchill's remarks are rude and libelous. *"Mr. Churchill maintains that Warsaw, Berlin, Prague, Vienna, Budapest, Belgrade, Bucharest, and Sofia, are within the Soviet sphere and are all subjected to Soviet influence and to the increasing control of Moscow."* Further, "*Mr. Churchill qualifies this as the 'boundless expansionist tendencies of the Soviet Union.' It requires no special effort to show that Mr. Churchill rudely and shamelessly libels not only Moscow but also the above-mentioned States neighborly to the U.S.S.R. To begin with, it is quite absurd to speak of the exclusive control of the U.S.S.R. in Vienna and Berlin, where there are Allied control councils with representatives of four States, where the U.S.S.R. has only one-fourth of the voices*" (the other three being the United States, France and Britain - qualifying comment added). Further, Stalin says: "*Secondly, ...the Germans carried out an invasion of the U.S.S.R. through Finland, Poland, Rumania, Bulgaria and Hungary....and were able to do so through these countries by reason of the fact that these countries had governments inimical to the Soviet Union.*" In other words, he seems to be alleging these countries allowed Germans to pass through to aggress the Soviet Union (or, as we might comment: were they simply so intimidated by Hitler that they wouldn't dare resist his desires? Furthermore, we might ask, were all these countries bordering the Soviet Union simply overridden, or conquered, by Hitler coincidental with his aggression against Russia?) Stalin goes on to claim that some seven million Soviet citizens were sent to "*German slave labor camps.*" He claims the Soviet Union lost in such manner more men that the United States and Britain combined. Very notably he says: "*It may be that some quarters are trying to push into oblivion these sacrifices of the Soviet people, which insured the liberation of Europe from the Hitlerite yoke.*"

There is more in this Pravda interview where Stalin took to task Churchill's accusations or claims regarding Soviet Russia's post-war aggressions. All of these Soviet rebuttals, which we feel seem reasonable, require scholarly review by experts on Soviet behavior in a complex world. For example, is/was Churchill correct in tagging Russia as a military threat after WW II, or was Soviet Russia in essence a victim of suspicion born of the way the disposition of the European nations shook out as a result of the end of WWII?

A few notable comments can be added here. On May 7, 1969, a large crowd gathered at Westminister College in Fulton, Missouri for the dedication of the Winston Churchill Memorial, where certainly in part, Churchill was remembered by one speaker, WWII British Admiral Lord Louis Mountbatten, for his words spoken March 5, 1946 (Iron Curtain speech) at Fulton. Another speaker at the dedication, United States Ambassador-at-Large W. Averell Harriman, was quoted in the St. Louis Globe-Democrat (May 8, 1969): " 'Churchill's words in 1946,' Harriman said, were 'an eloquent and true explanation of the realities of the situation ....the hard facts that had to be faced.' Harriman recalled his own meeting with Stalin one time after the war when the Soviet leader declared his intentions 'to take over Europe through Communist subversion.' " (p. 3A)

"The Darkening International Scene" Speech [5]

Delivered by Winston Churchill at the Waldorf Astoria Hotel, New York, March 15, 1946

This may well be the most definitive speech of Churchill following his March 5 "Iron Curtain" declaration. It confirms Churchill's resolve to proclaim his message in the face of Stalin's accusations made in the March 8 - 10 Pravda interview. According to a foreword regarding Churchill's March 15 address as published by R. R. James [5] : *"Churchill's Fulton speech had aroused a storm. Pravda had denounced him and accused him of trying to destroy the United Nations; Stalin had declared that Churchill called for war against the Soviet Union; in the House of Commons, Prime Minister Attlee pointedly declined comment on 'a speech delivered in another country by a private individual.' Meanwhile, the continued presence of Russian troops in Iran was the subject of an appeal by the Iranian Government to the U. N. Security Council. Churchill was unrepentant, and in this speech he set out to clarify his position."*

At the outset of this speech in New York, Churchill says he does not wish to withdraw or modify a single word he spoke in Fulton ten days before. He continues to advocate an *"increasing association"* [comment - perhaps he was careful not to use the words "military alliance"] between Britain and the United States [comment - a troubling aspect to his speech is that the suggested wedding between the United States and Britain would appear to exclude the Soviet Union, a nation among the ranks of the Allies during WWII; though later in his speech he invites, or leaves the door open, for Russia to join, should they show an interest - maintaining that but a few leaders in Russia would be responsible for making such an important decision]. Further along in his speech, he suggests that the Soviet Union *".....should take an honored place in the van of the World Organization."* Yet he says, *"Whether she will do so or not depends only on the decisions taken by a handful of able men who, under their renowned chief, hold the 180 million Russians, and many more millions outside Russia, in their grip."* [In my view, these words imply tyranny on the part of the Soviets, and whether true or not, in effect they further antagonize Soviet Russian leaders.] Churchill does not believe the rulers in Russia wish for war at this time. [comment - then why even mention war if he is not suggesting such a thing was probable or even possible? Either he is provoking a war- like mentality or alleging such a threat exists, based upon his esoteric understanding of the world's situation - which we cannot dismiss as reasonably to be ascribed to him, given his vast experience and understanding. It is an enormous task for scholars and military experts to understand the truthful intents of nations of the world and their leaders. They may say one thing, while pursuing any course of action deemed appropriate to their interests.]

Churchill ascribes great power to the United States post-WWII, while indicating that the United States and Britain, working together to strengthen the United Nations, could lend great authority to the U. N. to preserve world peace. He again says the "English-speaking" people, as people apart from the remainder of the world, are powerful, and in this he might be accused of suggesting some sort of world control by such. This appears to be the way Stalin interprets it, or casts his spin on Churchill's wedding of English-speaking people.

As if to bolster his assertion of Russian tyranny, Churchill uses the situation in contemporary Iran, which nation is occupied by the Russian military. Churchill claims that by agreements at the Potsdam conference (July-August, 1945), the United States, Britain and Russia were to pull out of Iran. And while the former two nations have pulled out, Russia remains as a military presence in Iran (Persia) as the case is due to go before the U.N. Security Council on March 25, 1946. [comment - Churchill seems to be alleging that the continued Russian presence in Iran constitutes evidence of Russia's world aggression.] Churchill acknowledges the great losses incurred by the Soviet Union in WWII, but at the same time says her gains have been great with the defeat of her two great enemies, Germany and Japan. The following is a notable quotation of Churchill to be remembered: *"Japan was overthrown almost entirely by American arms."* Further, he says that Russia recovered all that the nation lost to Japan forty years ago. Churchill claims that certain major water ways that should be free to international passage, are in fact under the potential of being closed at the discretion of a single nation, Russia. Churchill seems to further antagonize Soviet Russia in claiming that the members of the ruling party in Russia are not elected by the citizens through a free electoral process as in the United States and Britain, thus rebuffing Stalin's charges of some significance to be ascribed to one party rule in the United States and Britain. Yet, in the United States, while the president may be of one party, the Congress may be well represented by variable party affiliation.

Churchill asserts the importance of British and American relationships as being critical to the efficacy of the United Nations. He says: *"Unless they work together, in full loyalty to the Charter, the organization of the United Nations will cease to have any reality. No one will be able to put his trust in it and the world will be left to the clash of nationalisms which have led us to two frightful wars.* ***I never asked for an Anglo-American military alliance or a treaty*** (emphasis added)." Rather he says he asked for fraternal association, free and voluntary. [In my view, considering Churchill's claims from various speeches in March 1946, there resides in his words a fine line between such concepts as military alliance, fraternal association, friendship, and working together between Britain and the United States, given the attendant language he employs to characterize the proposed relationships between the two nations. It is not unreasonable for Stalin to construe, or put his spin on (if he wished to do so), Churchill's words to the effect that Churchill is actually speaking of military alliance; or ascribing such to the British - American relationship posed by Churchill.] In Churchill's concluding words, he says: *"We in the British Commonwealth will stand at your side in powerful and faithful friendship..."*

"A BROADER AND FAIRER WORLD" SPEECH[6]

Delivered by Winston Churchill at Columbia University, New York, March 18, 1946

This speech given at Columbia University is very brief as published in James (1974). It is but seven short paragraphs, and is hardly of such length as one would expect Winston Churchill to deliver at a major university. What's more, at the beginning of the third paragraph, one sees the following: "*...One thing the GI's and British soldiers returning home - etc., etc.,*" where, in my view, the initial three dots suggest other words were delivered by Churchill that were not reproduced in this publication. Similarly, at the terminus of the seventh (and last) paragraph, one finds: "*—the Governments of great States?...;*" the three dots similarly suggesting possible Churchill text not recorded in this publication of the speech. I may be mistaken in my interpretation that text from his speech was not recorded. Keeping this in mind, as to the text presented in this publication, the following might be said: According to Churchill, post-WWII, we must look forward to a "*broader, fairer world*" secured by the authority of a world organization [i.e. United Nations Organization (UNO)] to guard "*.....the humble toiler, the small homes of all nations, from renewed horrors and tyranny.*" He again suggests that Britain and the United States, in walking together, can secure the blessings for all people, presumably through support of the UNO. In speaking of the threat of tyranny to be guarded against by the UNO, in light of claims in his other speeches, there is a presumption that Soviet Russia may be the source of such tyranny, though in this speech, while he mentions Communists, there is so specific reference to the Soviet Union.

Churchill speaks of the close relationships between British and American soldiers during WWII, so close that soldiers of each nation developed a "*good grounding*" in "*Anglo-American slang,*" yet now as we move forward the two nations in working together must become familiar with the true "*mother tongues*" of the two nations, holding that there is "*great majesty and power*" in these languages. Similarly, we must mutually share the history of both nations. He speaks of the study of "*Anglo-American*" history. Churchill's last sentence reads: "*How can the one individual (meaning the humble common toiler in any nation) confront scores of problems and adjust himself to the position into which he is forced by tyrants who from time to time seize upon the Governments of great States?...*" [In my view there is more a shadow in this speech of his former assaults upon the Soviet Union appearing in others of his speeches such as the "Iron Curtain" speech in Fulton; yet, given those other speeches, this speech might be interpreted as furthering his concerns regarding Communism and the behavior (or potential behavior) of the Soviet Union.

Taken together, all of the March, 1946 speeches on the heels of the end of WWII, show a very substantial conflict emerging on the world stage among the Allied victors of WWII. This appears to have been born of Winston Churchill's "Iron Curtain" speech of March 5, 1946, in Fulton, Missouri - yet the stage for the content of this speech was set immediately after WWII, or before, as the war was winding down. A response by Stalin in Pravda, only served to enhance what appears to be a conflict between the "free world" and Communism - that went on to what became known as the "Cold War" between the Soviet Union and the West.

Suffice it to say, that during this turmoil that emerged during March 1946, while Churchill and members of his family were on vacation in the United States, it fell to Frank Dementi on March 8, 1946, in Richmond and Williamsburg, to have the exquisite opportunity to photograph the visiting party, which included former Supreme Allied Commander, General Dwight Eisenhower, and his wife Mamie, in both the public settings in Richmond and Williamsburg, and as the sole photographer or journalist invited into the private social gathering at Williamsburg's Raleigh Tavern. In the Raleigh Tavern, Frank Dementi's photographs, alone, recorded the great fellowship that existed among the party members. We, members of Frank's family, hold that Frank's photos of Winston Churchill, his wife Clementine Churchill, General Dwight Eisenhower, his wife Mamie Eisenhower, and other members of the visiting party, are the most interesting outstanding photographs of a controversial period in history. His photos of the "iron curtain" Churchill, and former Supreme Allied Commander, General Dwight Eisenhower, sharing cocktails in the Raleigh Tavern are among the most notable. Also, we claim his outstanding photographs of women who were a very important part of this event, constitute an additional singular contribution of Frank Dementi. Further, this time of harsh accusations being bandied back and forth by world leaders, which amounted to the inception of the cold war, was occurring precisely at the moment Frank took his photographs. The photographs themselves then take on enhanced meaning (rareness) as not only works of art, but as a photographic and journalistic record of that trying post-WWII time, which later ended with the tearing down of the Berlin Wall under President Ronald Reagan.

Brian Dementi, Ph.D.

Sources of Information

1. Copy of Churchill's speech, March 5, 1946. Churchill Truman Day collection, Winston Churchill Memorial Library in the United States, Westminster College (obtained by personal examination of the library's files in Fulton)
2. *Journal of the Joint Assembly of the General Assembly of the Commonwealth of Virginia, March 9, 1946, House Document No. 25,* pp. 10 - 17.
3. *Winston S. Churchill His Complete Speeches 1897 - 1963,* Ed. Robert Rhodes James (1974), Vol. VII 1943-1949, Chelsea House Publishers in association with R.R. Bowker Company, New York and London. p.7296 . (may be found in the Virginia State Library)
4. *Stalin Interview With Pravda On Churchill.* **New York Times**, March 14, 1946
5. *Winston S. Churchill His Complete Speeches 1897 - 1963,* Ed. Robert Rhodes James (1974), Vol. VII 1943-1949, Chelsea House Publishers in association with R.R. Bowker Company, New York and London. p. 7299.
6. *Winston S. Churchill His Complete Speeches 1897 - 1963,* Ed. Robert Rhodes James (1974), Vol. VII 1943-1949, Chelsea House Publishers in association with R.R. Bowker Company, New York and London. p. 7302.

Other references consulted:

Fulton Daily Sun-Gazette.
Atlee Says Briton Spoke For Himself. March 11, 1946, p. 1

New York Times, March 15, 1946
Acheson, Pleading Urgent Matter, Won't Speak at Churchill Dinner
Oppose Churchill Policy - Columbia Students in Peace Group to Hold Protest Rally
Schedule for Churchill

New York Times, March 16, 1946
Churchill Again Asks Anglo-U.S. Harmony
Puts Onus On Soviet If It Bars Cooperation
Iran To Appeal To UNO
Russians Press On
The City Pays Tribute To Britain's Wartime Prime Minister
Pickets In CIO Line Taunt Churchill
Text Of Speech by Churchill at Dinner Given in His Honor by City
Churchill Renews U.S. Unity Plea

NBC
NBC
WRNL

APPENDICES

Appendix 1

Itinerary for the visit of Winston Churchill to the United States: January - March, 1946

January 9	Winston and Clementine Churchill depart London on the Queen Elizabeth.
January 14	Winston and Clementine Churchill arrive in New York aboard the Queen Elizabeth; Churchill gives a press conference on arrival.
January 15	Churchills travel by train to Miami for six week vacation. Stay at home of Colonel Frank Clarke (5905 North Bay Road, Miami Beach, Florida).
January 17	Churchill and host Frank Clarke lunch with Lt. General Walter Bedell Smith, former Chief of Staff for General Dwight Eisenhower and Eisenhower's designee to sign the May 7, 1945 unconditional surrender of Germany.
January 18	Winston and Clementine Churchill go sight-seeing in Miami and visit a "parrot jungle."
February 1	Mr. and Mrs. Churchill visit the Hialeah Park Race Track.
February 2	Winston and Clementine Churchill and Colonel Frank Clarke depart at 1:15 P.M. for Cuba in a B17 airplane provided by President Harry Truman. They will be guests of the Cuban government. The Churchill's first act in Cuba is to call on the President Ramon Grau San Martin.

February 2	In Cuba, Churchill posts a letter from the Hotel Nacional de Cuba responding to an invitation from the Virginia General Assembly to address that body.
February 2	Sarah Churchill Oliver arrives in New York on the way to join her parents in Cuba after her first flight experienced engine trouble and was forced to return to London.
February 8	Churchills leave Havana, Cuba, to fly back to Miami.
February 10	Churchill and Colonel Clarke fly to Washington to meet President Truman in the White House. Conference said to be about plans for the speech at Westminster College with no discussion about the pending $4,000,000,000 loan to Britain.
February 11	Churchill visits with retiring British ambassador, Lord Halifax at the British Embassy in Washington D.C.
February 12	Churchill and Colonel Clarke fly back to Miami in company with Marshall Field, a Chicago publisher.
February 16	Churchill visited in Miami by Secretary of State James Byrnes and presidential advisor, financier Bernard Baruch. March 5 speech at Westminster College is topic of conversation.
February 26	Churchill awarded honorary Doctor of Laws Degree by the University of Miami at the Orange Bowl Stadium.
February 27	Mr. Churchill sits again for artist Douglas Chandor to paint a portrait. Mr. Chandor had already painted President Franklin Roosevelt, and planned to visit Russia to paint Stalin, but he died before he could bring to fruition Roosevelt's dream of portraits of all three participants in the Yalta Conference of February, 1945.
March 1	Miami Surf Club farewell luncheon for the Churchills.

March 2 Churchill with his wife, Clementine, daughter, Sarah Oliver, and host Colonel Frank Clarke travel in a private rail car to Washington for a stay in the White House. They are met at Union Station in Washington by reporter/son Randolph Churchill.

March 4-5 Mr. Churchill and President Truman travel by presidential train to Fulton, Missouri.

March 5 Mr Churchill delivers address,*The Sinews of Peace,* at Westminster College in Fulton, Missouri, where he also receives an honorary degree.

March 5-7 Mr. Churchill (and party) returns to Washington by train. (President Truman returns separately by plane.)

March 8 Mr. Churchill and General Dwight Eisenhower (and party) travel by presidential train from Washington to Richmond, Virginia.

March 8 Mr Churchill delivers scheduled speech, *The English-Speaking Peoples,* in A.M. to Virginia General Assembly. By popular demand General Eisenhower delivers impromptu address to General Assembly They and their party of about 12 persons then travel to Colonial Williamsburg for a tour of the restored area, a social and a dinner, leaving Williamsburg by train at midnight to return to Washington, D.C.

March 9 Mr. Churchill delivers address, *The Anglo-American Alliance,* at the Pentagon in Northern Virginia.

March 11 Mr. Churchill is a guest at a press luncheon sponsored by the Overseas Writers Association. He then departs Washington along with his family, for New York City after a 15 minute call on Truman in the White House to say farewell. They stay at the Hotel Waldorf-Astoria in New York.

March 12 Mr. and Mrs. Churchill, daughter Sarah, Frank Clarke, and John Winant, U.S. Ambassador to the Court of St. James, visit Franklin Roosevelt's grave at Hyde Park and lunch there with Eleanor Roosevelt. That evening, Mr. Churchill and Colonel Clarke have dinner with Governor and Mrs. Dewey at the Executive Mansion in Albany, New York.

March 15 Mr. Churchill delivers address, *The Darkening International Scene,* at a civic luncheon at the Hotel Waldorf-Astoria, New York.

March 18 Mr. Churchill delivers address, *A Broader and Fairer World,* at Colombia University, New York.

March 21 Churchills begin their return trip to England on the Queen Mary

.

Sources of Information

Fulton Daily Sun-Gazette

Churchill Interviewed On Arrival. January 16, 1946, p. 2.
Winston Churchill to Speak In Fulton. March 5; Truman Coming. December 19, 1945, p. 1.
Churchill Goes on a Sight-seeing Tour. January 18, 1946, p. 2.
Kiss From Cockatoo. January 31, 1946, p. 2.
Joins Parents (Arrival of Sarah Churchill in U.S.) February 4, 1946, p. 1.
Churchills Leave Cuba. February 8, 1946, p. 2.
Churchill, Truman Confer On Trip. February 11, 1946, p. 1.
Churchill Returns To Miami, Fla., By Plane. February 13, 1946, p. 2.
Announce Party's Travel Schedule. February 26, 1946, p. 1.
Churchill On Way To Washington. March 2, 1946. p. 1.
Truman, Churchill Leave for Missouri. March 4, 1946, p. 1.
Churchill Arrives in Washington After Tour. March 7, 1946, p. 2.

Packwood, Allen, Director of the Churchill Archives Centre, Churchill College, Cambridge, England,
personal communication

Richmond News Leader
Churchill Basks in Florida Sun. January 17, 1946, p. 13.
Havana Plans Public Drive for Churchill. January 30, 1946, p. 20.
Churchill Leaves for First Visit to Cuba in 50 Years. February 1, 1946, Blue Streak Edition, p. 1.
Churchill Visits The Races. February 1, 1946, p. 1-B.
Churchill Plans Call On Truman - To Be At White House At 8:30 P.M. Sunday. February 2, 1946, p. 1.
Churchills Plan to Leave U. S. March 21. February 27, 1946, p. 1

Richmond Times Dispatch
Speaking Dates Held to One By Churchill. January 16, p. 10.
Vacationing Churchill Breezes through City. January 16, 1946, p. 3
Churchill, Smith Recall D-Day Thrills. January 18, 1946, p. 6.
Churchill Paints 'Topnotch' Oil. January 19, 1946, p. 4.
Daughter's Danger Keeps Churchills Close to Phone. February 1, 1946, p. 4.
Winston Churchill Returns to Miami. February 9, 1946, p. 1.
Churchill Will Visit White House. February 10, 1946, p. 7.
Churchill Talks With Truman After Flight From Florida. February 11, 1946, pp. 1, 2.
Churchill Party Return to Florida. February 13, 1946, p. 4.
Byrnes, Baruch Visit Churchill. February 17, 1946, p. 1.
Churchill Stresses Care of Veterans. February 27, 1946, p. 4.
U. S. British Alliance Urged by Churchill; Soviet Policy Scored. March 6, 1946, pp. 1, 4.
Churchill Leaves Washington After Paying Farewell Visits. March 12, 1946, p. 3.
Churchill Places Wreath On Tomb Of Roosevelt. March 13, 1946, p. 5.

Appendix II

Senate Joint Resolution No. 6

Inviting the Honorable Winston Spencer Churchill to address the General Assembly of Virginia

———————

Patrons: Messrs Brock and Battle

———————

"WHEREAS, during England's darkest hours in World War II her great Prime Minister, the Honorable Winston Spencer Churchill, with matchless eloquence and indomitable will, inspired his bomb-scarred nation to fight on until the resources and weight of the democratic nations could be mustered to overthrow the ruthless conqueror; and

"WHEREAS, by his patience and understanding, and his ability to work with other great leaders in the cause of freedom, Winston Churchill helped to weld together in an invincible military union the British Empire, the Soviet Union, and the United States of America, and thereby insured the destruction of the Axis powers, the liberation of prostrate Europe, and the survival of civilization itself; and

"WHEREAS, because of his American mother, the beautiful and accomplished Jenny Jerome, and his many personal ties with our country, the presence of Winston Churchill in the United States is a source of satisfaction, not only to the few who know him as an intimate and well-loved friend, but to the many who look upon him as one of history's immortals; now therefore,

"BE IT RESOLVED by the Senate of Virginia, the House of Delegates concurring, that the General Assembly of Virginia, the oldest lawmaking body in the Western Hemisphere, hereby invites the Honorable Winston Spencer Churchill to appear before it at such time as may suit his convenience, and to address it upon such subject as he may deem appropriate; and

"BE IT FURTHER RESOLVED, that the Clerk of the Senate transmit a copy of this resolution to the Honorable Winston Spencer Churchill upon his arrival in the State of Florida."

(Agreed to January 16, 1946)

As printed in the **Journal of the Joint Assembly of the General Assembly of the Commonwealth of Virginia March 8, 1946 House Document No. 25,** pp. 24 - 25.

APPENDIX III

FEBRUARY 13 LETTER FROM WINSTON CHURCHILL TO GOVERNOR WILLIAM TUCK

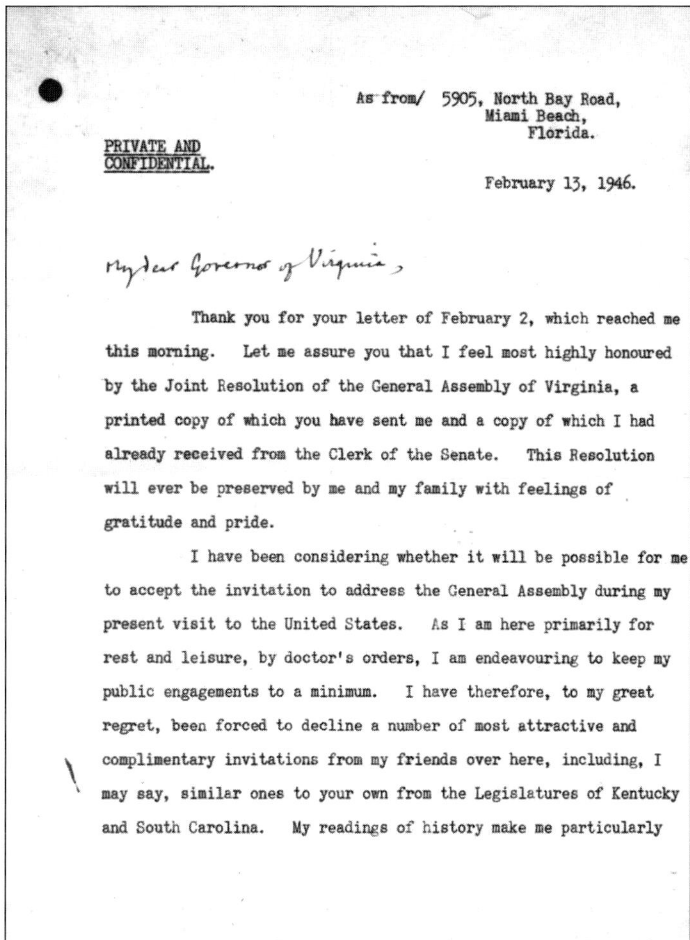

As from/ 5905, North Bay Road,
Miami Beach,
Florida.

PRIVATE AND
CONFIDENTIAL.

February 13, 1946.

My dear Governor of Virginia,

Thank you for your letter of February 2, which reached me this morning. Let me assure you that I feel most highly honoured by the Joint Resolution of the General Assembly of Virginia, a printed copy of which you have sent me and a copy of which I had already received from the Clerk of the Senate. This Resolution will ever be preserved by me and my family with feelings of gratitude and pride.

I have been considering whether it will be possible for me to accept the invitation to address the General Assembly during my present visit to the United States. As I am here primarily for rest and leisure, by doctor's orders, I am endeavouring to keep my public engagements to a minimum. I have therefore, to my great regret, been forced to decline a number of most attractive and complimentary invitations from my friends over here, including, I may say, similar ones to your own from the Legislatures of Kentucky and South Carolina. My readings of history make me particularly

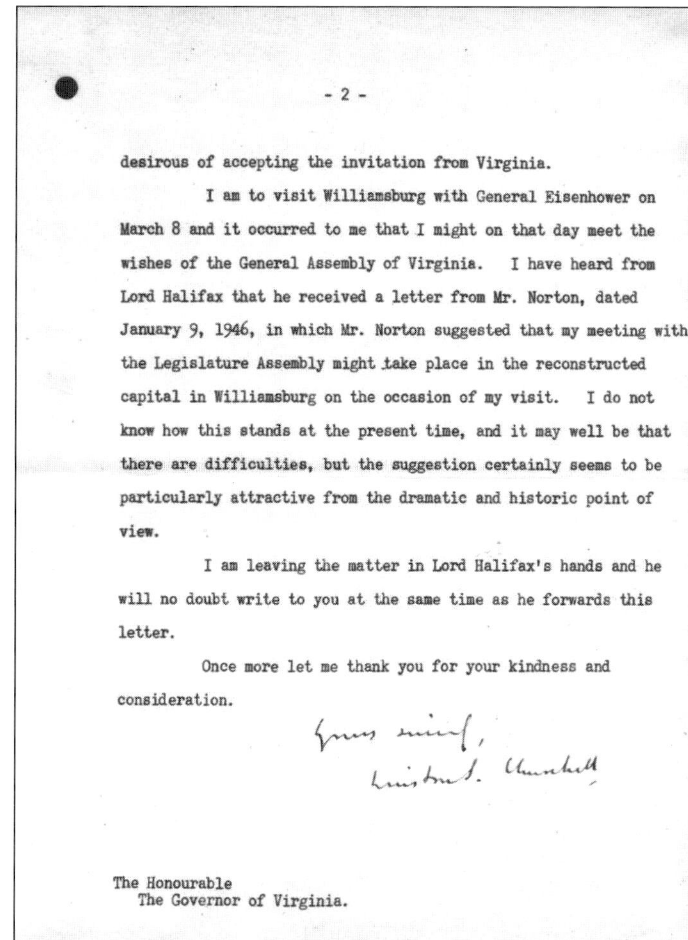

- 2 -

desirous of accepting the invitation from Virginia.

I am to visit Williamsburg with General Eisenhower on March 8 and it occurred to me that I might on that day meet the wishes of the General Assembly of Virginia. I have heard from Lord Halifax that he received a letter from Mr. Norton, dated January 9, 1946, in which Mr. Norton suggested that my meeting with the Legislature Assembly might take place in the reconstructed capital in Williamsburg on the occasion of my visit. I do not know how this stands at the present time, and it may well be that there are difficulties, but the suggestion certainly seems to be particularly attractive from the dramatic and historic point of view.

I am leaving the matter in Lord Halifax's hands and he will no doubt write to you at the same time as he forwards this letter.

Once more let me thank you for your kindness and consideration.

Yours sincerely,
Winston S. Churchill

The Honourable
The Governor of Virginia.

From: Governor William M. Tuck, Executive Papers (Legislature), 1946. Box number 120. Accession #24026. The Library of Virginia. Used with permission

APPENDIX IV

TEXT OF WINSTON CHURCHILL'S ADDRESS TO THE VIRGINIA GENERAL ASSEMBLY, MARCH 8, 1946

As printed in the Journal of the Joint Assembly of the General Assembly of the Commonwealth of Virginia (House Document No. 25)

"*Mr. Speaker, Members of the Joint Assembly of Virginia, Ladies and Gentlemen:*

"I was deeply moved by the glowing terms of the joint resolution of both branches of the Legislature inviting me here to address the General Assembly of Virginia. I take it as a high honor to be present here this morning to discharge that task.

"Now I always value being asked to address a parliament. I have already on two occasions in the war addressed the Congress of the United States. I have addressed the Canadian Parliament. I have addressed a joint session of the Belgian Legislature more recently. And there is a place of which you may have heard across the ocean, called the House of Commons, to which invited or uninvited, I have from time to time had things to say. *[Laughter.]*

"I have also had invitations couched in terms for which I am most grateful from the State Legislatures of South Carolina, Kentucky and Mississippi. It would have given me the very greatest pleasure to accept and fulfill all these, but as I have not the life and strength to repay all the kindness which is offered me, I felt that these other States would be willing to accept the primacy of the Virginia Assembly as the most ancient lawmaking body on the mainland of the Western Hemisphere. And thus, I find myself here before you this morning in Richmond, the historic capital of world-famous Virginia. *[Applause.]*

"I am also about to visit Williamsburg. During the war at one of our conferences, General Marshall arranged to take the British Chiefs of the Staff for a visit to Williamsburg and I had planned to go with them, but the work I had to do made it necessary for me to remain in Washington, and so on this visit to the United States, I promised myself the treat of seeing Williamsburg. And my friend, General Eisenhower, who is with us today, undertook to pilot me around. I have great satisfaction in meeting him over here. We had a lot of business to do together during what I believe has been called in another connection 'the late unpleasantness', [laughter] and I have formed impressions that will last me all my days, of his single-hearted purpose, his wide and profound views on military science, and his great power of making the soldiers and officers of our two countries work together under all the shocks and strains of war as if they were the soldiers of one single nation. *[Applause.]*

"I hope I shall acquit myself today to your satisfaction *[Laughter.]* But the responsibility for what may happen, Mr. Speaker, it is yours. Do you not think you are running some risk in inviting me to give my faithful counsel on this occasion? You have not asked to see beforehand what I am going to say. I might easily, for instance, blurt out a lot of things which people know in their hearts are true, but are a bit shy in saying in public. *[Laughter.]* And this might cause a regular commotion and get you all into trouble. However, the people of Virginia, and above all the people of Richmond, have proved in the past that they have strong nerves, and that they can face not only facts, but fate, with fortitude and pride.

"Of course, Sir, my mind goes back into the past, so much of which we have in common. The light of the Elizabethan age, which Shakespeare, Raleigh, and Grenville adorned, casts its unfading luster upon our scene here and in Williamsburg nearby. This was a cradle of the great republic in which more than a hundred and fifty years afterwards the strong champions of freedom and independence were found to have been nursed.

"With what care, Mr. Speaker, did those early fathers of our modern inspiration preserve the title deeds of freedom, in parliamentary privilege, in trial by jury, in the habeas corpus, in Magna Carta, and in the English common law. With what vigilance did Thomas Jefferson, Patrick Henry with his 'give me liberty or give me death', and Robert* Henry Lee, and above all, George Washington, the father of his country, defend these title deeds in later unhappy but pregnant times.

"The theme of individual liberty and of the rights of the citizen so painfully evolved across the centuries in England was upheld through every stress and confusion by Virginia, and that theme lights the English speaking world today. It lights our world and it is also a beacon shining through the mists and storms to many lands where the rights of man, his honor, his happiness, his freedom are yearned for, or are so far enjoyed only precariously. Mr. Speaker, I salute you here in this General Assembly, as the guardians of the sacred flame.

---

* *Richard Henry Lee*

"Another century passes across our minds and we see Virginia and Richmond at the center of a tragedy, which however agonizing at the time is now forever illuminated by drama and romance. And I have visited most of your battlefields on the Peninsula, on the Rappahannock, in the Wilderness, and I was guided there some years ago by your distinguished historian, Mr. Freeman, who I believe is here today, and whose works are a solid contribution not only to the fame of the South but to the whole strength of the indissoluble American Union.

"Yet it is in the words of an English general officer that I shall express myself to you this morning. General Henderson, the author of 'The Life of Stonewall Jackson' and 'The Campaign of Fredericksburg,' was a man I knew nearly forty years ago. And this is what he wrote:

> *Far and wide between the mountains and the sea stretches the fair Virginia, for which Lee and Jackson and their soldiers, one equal temper of heroic hearts, fought so well and unavailingly. Yet her brows are bound with glory, the legacy of her lost children; and her spotless name uplifted by their victories and manhood is high among the nations. Surely she may rest content, knowing that so long as men turn to the records of history will their deeds live, giving to all time one of the noblest examples of unyielding courage and devotion the world has known. [Applause.]*

"Mr. Speaker, my grandfather was a Northerner in the State of New York, and you would not expect me to belie the cause for which he strove. We have moved on into a broader age and larger combinations. Old battles are remembered not as sources of bitterness but to celebrate the martial virtues and civic fidelity of both sides in that immortal struggle. Out of this story have also come examples of high character in which Americans have shown themselves in nowise wanting under the new trials and tribulations through which we have passed.

"There was about General Robert E. Lee a character, a quality of selflessness which raises him to the very highest rank of men, whether soldiers or statesmen, who are being concerned with the fortunes of nations, *[applause]* and in General Marshall and General Eisenhower and others of the Army and Navy of the United States whom I could mention, that character, that quality of selflessness has been a bond uniting allied armies and the key to the victory which we have gained together. *[Applause.]*

"Today the American Union is the most powerful champion of national and individual freedom, and it carries with it a large portion of the hopes of men. All the world wonders at the prodigious exertions of the United States in the late struggle when she was carrying on at the same time two major wars against two first-class, long-prepared military powers - one in the East another in the West and both across two wide oceans - and when she also acted as the great arsenal of democracy to the friends of freedom in every land. *[Applause.]*

"It has been said, Mr. Speaker, that the dominant lesson of history, it is that mankind is unteachable. You will remember how my dear friend, the late President Roosevelt, had to argue only a few years ago that Americans were not what is called 'soft' and how he asserted that this was 'the land of unending challenge,' and I myself have read in secret documents, German reports which spoke of, before they met them, of 'these ridiculous Americans troops.' Surely these European countries should not have forgotten or ignored so soon the examples of tenacity, willpower, and self-devotion which shine through all the records of the great war between the American States. We, too, on our British Island and in our great, self-governing empire spread about the world, have proved that our race when stirred to its depths has qualities deserving of respect. *[Applause.]*

"In fact, in proportion to our numbers, our efforts, our output, our sacrifices and losses have not been surpassed. Moreover, it fell to us to have the honor of standing alone for a whole year against the main strength of the mighty Axis, and the time for preparations which was thus gained, was, as I am sure General Eisenhower will agree, of vital service to the United States and to the common cause. *[Applause.]*

"But it is upon the future rather than upon the past that I wish to rest this morning. In these last years of my life there is a message of which I conceive myself to be the bearer. It is a very simple message which can be well understood by the people of both our countries. It is that we should stand together. *[Applause.]* We should stand together in malice to none, in greed for nothing, but in defense of those causes which we hold dear. Not only for our own benefit, but because we believe they mean the honor and the happiness of long generations of men. *[Applause.]* We ought, as I said to the Congress of the United States in a dark hour in 1941, to walk together in majesty and peace. That, I am sure, is the wish of the overwhelming majority of the 200 million Britons and Americans who are spread about the globe. That is, that this is our destiny, or, as most of us would put it, the will of God, seems sure and certain. How it is to be expressed, in what way and in what hour it is to be achieved, I cannot tell.

"I read, Mr. Speaker, the other day that an English nobleman, whose name is new to me, had stated that England would have to become the forty-ninth State of the American Union. *[Laughter.]* I read yesterday that an able American editor had written that the United States ought not to be asked to re-enter the British Empire. *[Laughter.]* But it seems to me, and I dare say it seems to you, that the path of wisdom lies somewhere between these scarecrow extremes. *[Laughter and applause.]* We must find the means and the method of working together not only in times of war and mortal anguish, but in times of peace with all its bewilderments and clamor and clatter of tongues.

"It is in the years of peace that wars are prevented and that those foundations are laid upon which the noble structures of the future can be built. But peace will not be preserved without the virtues that make victory possible in war. Peace will not be preserved by pious sentiments expressed in terms of platitudes or by official grimaces and diplomatic correctitude however desirable these may be from time to time. It will not be preserved by casting aside in dangerous years the panoply of warlike strength. There must be earnest thought. There must also be faithful perseverance and foresight. Great Heart must have his sword and armor to guard the pilgrims on their way. Above all, among the English speaking peoples there must be the union of hearts based upon conviction and common ideals. That is what I offer. That is what I seek. *[Prolonged applause]*"

Text of General Dwight Eisenhower's extemporaneous address to the Virginia General Assembly, March 8, 1946

As printed in the Journal of the Joint Assembly of the General Assembly of the Commonwealth of Virginia (House Document No. 25)

"Ladies and Gentleman:

"It is one of the high honors of my life to return to a joint meeting of the Legislature in the State in which my mother was born and reared. *[Applause.]* I could not conceive of a happier occasion upon which to come than as one of the aides of one of the great men of the world, - *[applause]* the man in whose indomitable spirit the Allies found inspiration during the war, the man whose conception of political, industrial, and military affairs led him to be the chief inspiration for the North African campaign and whose battle spirit never wavered for one single second in support of any time that the fight was joined by sea, by air, or by land. *[Applause.]*

"Of all the things that supported me through three and a half years of warfare on the European continent, I know of no other single thing that was of greater moral benefit than the unwavering, staunch, indomitable, courageous support of the Prime Minister of Great Britain. *[Applause.]* It is my earnest conviction that only history can measure even remotely the true value of the worth of the service he has rendered to all of us. But I am certain that in meetings such as this with the wholehearted welcome he finds in this city from my own countrymen to him, he will gain some little measure of understanding in his own time, of what we think of him. Thank you. *[Applause.]*"

APPENDIX V

MENU* FOR DINNER GIVEN BY MR. AND MRS. JOHN D. ROCKEFELLER, III IN HONOR OF WINSTON CHURCHILL AND GENERAL DWIGHT EISENHOWER

Williamsburg Inn, Colonial Williamsburg, March 8, 1946, 8:30 P.M.

Crabmeat Cocktail, Claridge Sauce
Dainty Beaten Biscuits, Buttered
Celery, Olives, Radishes
Terrapin a la Maryland
Cheese Straws
Fried Chicken, Cream Gravy
Sweet Potato Souffle Fresh Asparagus, Hollandaise
Sally Lunn Bread Assorted Relishes
Mixed Green Salad
French Dregoing, with Olive Oil and Aromatic Herbs
Virginia Ham
Bel Paese Cheese
Fresh Strawberry Ice Cream
with Homemade Assorted Cakes
Demi Tasse
Fruits, Salted Nuts, After Dinner Mints
Cigars - Dunhill's Monte Cristo, Number 3
Wines:
Cochran Sherry
Louis Roederer Champagne, Extra Dry, 1928
Martel's Cordon Bleu Brandy
Bisquit Dubouche Brandy
Veritable Benedictino, Liqueor
"Billancourt," Creme de Menthe
Van der Hum South African Liqueor

* *Menu courtesy of Joan Apter, daughter of John Green, caterer of the dinner*

THE END

Dr. Brian A. and Patricia (Pat) Long Dementi are native Richmonders, both born in Johnston Willis Hospital on Kensington Avenue. They met in a science class at the University of Richmond after Brian graduated from Hampden-Sydney College, and each pursued a graduate degree at the Medical College of Virginia.

The elder son of Frank Dementi, Brian was eight when his father had the exclusive opportunity to photograph Churchill and Eisenhower in the Raleigh Tavern in Williamsburg on March 8, 1946. But he grew up repeatedly hearing Frank's stories of the event. After a career as a biochemist and toxicologist, the last twenty-five years spent at the Environmental Protection Agency in Washington, D.C., he has devoted much of his retirement to his grandchildren, to singing at his church, and to cataloguing and "informing" his father's photos, with a goal of publishing the pictures, their context, and Frank's stories. This book represents the first and perhaps the most comprehensive of several publications.

Pat joined the Dementi family in 1967. After the birth of children Briana and Frank Dorset, she taught biology at Randolph-Macon College in Ashland, Virginia, for twenty-eight years. In retirement, she has devoted her time to grandchildren Bennett and Addison, to her second career (sewing doll clothes), and to helping Brian in various ways in the publication effort.